MW01273814

WHERE THEIR WORM
DOES NOT DIE
AND FIRE IS NOT QUENCHED

SHRADHA S. PHILIP

CREATION
HOUSE

WHERE THEIR WORM DOES NOT DIE AND FIRE IS NOT QUENCHED by
Shradha S. Philip
Published by Creation House
A Charisma Media Company
600 Rinehart Road
Lake Mary, Florida 32746
www.charismamedia.com

Unless otherwise noted, all Scripture quotations are from New King
James Version of the Bible. Copyright © 1979, 1980, 1982 by Thomas
Nelson, Inc., publishers. Used by permission.

Scripture quotations marked KJV are from the King James Version of
the Bible.

Scripture quotations marked NIV are from the Holy Bible, New
International Version. Copyright © 1973, 1978, 1984, 2010, 2011,
International Bible Society. Used by permission.

Scripture quotations marked NLT are from the Holy Bible, New Living
Translation, copyright © 1996. Used by permission of Tyndale House
Publishers, Inc., Wheaton, IL 60189. All rights reserved.

Scripture quotations marked NAS are from the New American Standard
Bible–Updated Edition, Copyright © 1960, 1962, 1963, 1968, 1971, 1972,
1973, 1975, 1977, 1995 by The Lockman Foundation. Used by permission.
(www.Lockman.org)

Design Director: Bill Johnson
Cover design by Nathan Morgan

Visit the author's website: www.warriorsinchrist.org

Library of Congress Cataloging-in-Publication Data: 2013941268
International Standard Book Number: 978-1-62136-389-7
E-book International Standard Book Number: 978-1-62136-390-3

First edition

13 14 15 16 17 — 9 8 7 6 5 4 3 2 1
Printed in Canada

DEDICATION

Dedicated for the glory and service of Jesus Christ who called me out of darkness into His wonderful light, without whom this book could never have been written.

He has stuck to me closer than a brother through all those years when I went through the deep waters and rivers of difficulty and walked through the fire of oppression.

And when I walked through the valley of shadow of death, He brought me back to the land of the living and breathed life into my nostrils that I may declare the praises of Him to all generations.

You have granted me life and favor, And Your care has pre-served my spirit.

—Job 10:12

TABLE OF CONTENTS

INTRODUCTION

THIS BOOK IS a factual account based on revelation of hell as revealed to me by the Lord Jesus Christ. This book is written in obedience to the direct command of the Lord Jesus Christ who specifically asked me to put these revelations in print to send out a warning to the world that hell is awfully real.

He said to me, "The very reason I have shown you so many hidden truths of hell in great depth is to share it with the world and warn them about the reality of hell. I do not desire that even one soul should perish. I gave My life as a ransom for their sins. People do not understand that if they do not have Me, they do not have life."

> He who has the Son has life; he who does not have the Son of God does not have life.
>
> —1 JOHN 5:12

"Daughter, warn them that hell is real."

> I have come to call the sinners to repentance.
>
> —LUKE 5:32

"Let them repent of their sins and live."

> For I have come not to condemn the world but that it might be saved through Me.
>
> —JOHN 3:17

My personal encounters with Jesus Christ began in the year 1995 at the time of pursuing a bachelor of arts degree at university. Since then He has taken me numerous times to heaven and hell.

I was taken to different parts of hell at times for days in a row and sometimes on individual days. The experiences described in chapters 6 and 7, "Warning for Future" and "A Glimpse of Hell," are both from 1995. In the year 2000 I was taken to the chamber of torment. In the months of April and May of the following year, 2001, Jesus took me continuously to different parts of hell and showed me the lost souls. In the year 2002 I was shown the fallen angels. In the later part of the same year, Satan visited me for the first time (mentioned in chapter 1, "Satan is a Real Adversary"). From the year 2003 to August of 2012, I was shown more. In May 2009 I was shown the abyss and the three chambers (chamber of apostasy and heresy, the occult chamber, and the chamber where secret pacts are made with Satan) for three nights in a row. In July 2012 I was shown the rest of the chambers on four consecutive nights.

From the period these trips to hell began until the book could be completed, an extraordinary thing happened that I believe was given of the Lord to increase my burden for the lost. At times when I saw pictures of those who were deceased (and these souls ended up in hell), I began to see them in the manner in which they died and burning in flames of fire screaming out for help. Once I was in a café and a picture of a woman who had since died adorned the wall. As soon as I looked at it, the picture of the woman disappeared and in its place I could see her burning in raging flames of fire and screaming out for help. Experiences of this sort continued to happen till this book could be completed. This has added to my commitment to see the lost saved.

My experiences in hell have proved to be an "eye opener" and a "myth buster." Though what I have been shown is immense, I have tried my best to record it all faithfully and describe everything to the best of my ability. I have not written this book with "persuasive words of human wisdom" (1 Cor. 2:4) but as revealed to me through the Spirit of God.

Dear reader, hell is a real place of continual, unexplainable affliction, with no chance of ever getting out. Everything I witnessed there is permanently engraved on my mind and will stay with me as long as I live.

Satan hates you and wants you to end up in hell. He has tried hard to dissuade me from exposing his lies and the reality of his kingdom, yet he has failed in all his attempts. He asked me to quit this divine commission, which I had already started to document from the year 2001 with a view to publish it one day as per the Lord's command. On his final visit, Satan said, "You have not paid heed to my previous warnings, so you will not live to complete this book." After this final warning an incident occurred (mentioned in chapter 1, "Satan Is a Real Adversary") in which I died and left my body, but God in His mercy brought me back for His glory. Since this incident He also went on to show me more about hell. This is a further proof that our Redeemer lives, and if not for Him I would not be alive today and you would not be reading this book. I live today to prove that hell exists and so does Satan. May your eyes be opened to this truth as you read this book.

If you do not have Jesus in your life, you are lost and certainly on your way to hell. If you can plan for holidays or short outings and even for picnics months in advance, it is unwise not to plan where you will spend your eternity, which is forever. There is a heaven and there is a hell. Please repent and accept Jesus Christ as your Savior now while there is hope. Tomorrow might be too late. What if death strikes you suddenly? Where will you end up—in heaven or hell? Are you prepared? Think about it.

Heaven or hell? It is your choice. I sincerely hope and pray that you will find Jesus Christ as you read this book, and choose heaven as your eternal abode.

Chapter One

SATAN IS A REAL ADVERSARY

IT IS IMPORTANT to know that Satan is a very real person as mentioned in the Bible in Isaiah 14:12–17 and Ezekiel 28:11–19. He is an adversary of God and His children. Jesus Christ also affirmed this fact. I can only accentuate this fact, recorded in the Bible centuries ago, to be the absolute truth as a result of my own firsthand experience with Satan.

This might sound incredible to you, nevertheless it is a fact: Satan visited me four times in person. His first visit was in December 2002. He asked me whether I would still serve Jesus if he took everything from me. He visited me again in May 2003, and twice in 2009 in the months of May and July. I saw him with my naked eyes, not in a vision or dream. On his second and third visits, he spoke to me in his desperate yet determined attempts to discourage me from writing this book about hell and told me repeatedly to quit this divine commission.

Please note: I had been recording my experiences of hell faithfully as asked by God from the year 2001 with the intention of publishing it one day. Satan spoke in reference to this. And on his final visit Satan tried to subjugate me by threatening me. He said, "You have not heeded to my previous warnings, so I have come to tell you that you will not live to complete this book." After this final encounter, he sought to kill me.

This following incident took place after this threat while I was on my way back to my destination after ministering. I had journeyed alone before numerous times but I did not have a slight inkling that this trip would prove to be different and remain memorable as a result.

In the dead of the night as I slept, being a light sleeper I was woken up by the sudden presence of an intruder. I saw death in front of my eyes. He came with a motive; not to rob or steal, but to kill.

This assailant thrust the blanket over my face covering it completely so that it blocked my breathing and then smothered me. He did it with such agility and expertise that took me by surprise. Apparently he was no novice but a master in this evil craft, and I was one of his victims.

I fought desperately for life, but after a while I gave up the struggle. It was at this point that I died and left my body. Hovering above my body, I looked at myself covered completely with the blanket, lying absolutely still and not breathing. I saw my assailant leave just as quickly as he came, certain of having claimed yet another victim and satisfied of having achieved his purpose. As soon as he left, I found myself back in my body mumbling, "Oh! I am breathing again," as I drew a breath for the first time after the incident.

> Satan is a thief that does not come except to steal, and to kill, and to destroy.
>
> —John 10:10

On two occasions prior to this incident, I have had close brushes with death. Apparently Satan had known that God has marked me for His glory.

The first time, I was an energetic three and one-half-year-old. I accidentally fell from the balcony of a second-floor apartment where we lived at the time. I fell right onto the rose garden below, and my head awkwardly rested between two sharp-edged bricks stacked horizontally that served as the border of the garden.

I was rushed to the hospital by my mother and kindhearted neighbors for a checkup. After examining me, the doctor on duty at the hospital refused to even believe my story of the accidental fall. Clearly mystified by my survival, given my age at the time of the fall from such height and with no visible internal or external injuries on the body—not even bruises—he asked in disbelief, "What is the proof that she fell from a second floor apartment?" It was only on the insistence of the kindhearted neighbors, witnesses to the event, who stood as "proof" along with my mother that the doctor accepted to believe the truth in the story. God saved me for a purpose, no doubt.

The second incident took place when I was in senior high school and was run over by the school bus. As I was about to get down from the bus at my usual stop, to my shock and disbelief, the driver accelerated the speed of the bus, which resulted in my tumbling out of the moving vehicle and landing beneath its wheels.

As the overwhelming feeling of certainty of death encompassed me, I shut my eyes, slipping unto unconsciousness expecting never to awaken again. After a while I regained consciousness, got up, and walked straight up to the bus stalled in the corner before turning to go home.

Amidst the chaos and looks of grave concern on the baffled faces of students and teachers alike on board in the bus, I was greeted with, "Oh! You are alive; we thought you were dead." I had been run over by the bus and should have been dead but I escaped with absolutely no injuries or repercussions of any sort, just like before. God had saved me again.

The enemy has done everything possible to keep me from writing this book, not to mention the unexplained delays up to the completion of writing this book. Besides that I have encountered a plethora of unexplained difficulties and undergone traumatic events, fiery oppressions, severe attacks, and been to the point of death many times and have lost all. Yet in spite of all his attempts, the enemy has not prevailed against me.

The good news is that Jesus Christ has rendered him powerless.

"Having disarmed principalities and powers, He made a public spectacle of them, triumphing over them in it" (Col. 2:15).

The very fact that I live today, against all odds, and you are holding this book in your hands is living proof that Jesus Christ is alive. He not only brought me back from the jaws of death to life, but He also went on to show me more about hell after the mentioned final incident.

Christians, be informed that Satan is your real enemy and you are engaged in real warfare with him. Stand your ground in Jesus Christ, equipped with His armor, fighting the good fight of faith, and you will overcome the enemy who walks about as a prowling lion, seeking whom he may devour (1 Pet. 5:8).

Chapter Two

WHAT HAPPENS WITH DEATH?

D EATH IS INEVITABLE and comes to all, irrespective of age whether young or old. The Bible likens it to a snare that befalls suddenly.

> For man does not know his time: Like fish taken in a cruel net, Like birds caught in a snare, So the sons of man are snared in an evil time, When it falls suddenly upon them.
> —ECCLESIASTES 9:12

I witnessed many lost souls of men and women on their way to hell. These lost souls, irrespective of their age whether young or old, were unprepared for their death that had come to them suddenly.

It is important to note that the earthbound spirits are a myth. These are demons in the guise of the deceased and appear in their forms and often mistaken as ghosts. These demons certainly do not need the help from mankind to cross over to the other side. This is a deception played on gullible and uninformed minds.

During my many trips to hell, I came across many such demons that appeared to people as ghosts. Beloved, you cannot be earth-bound because you do not want to leave this earth after your death. It is impossible to stick around on earth after death. This is clearly mentioned in the Bible: "And as it is appointed for men to die once, but after this the judgment" (Heb. 9:27).

I saw lost souls compelled to continue that terror-bound journey on the path in darkness much against their will to their doom.

If you live your life on this earth without Jesus Christ and die in that state, you will find the following happening to you simultaneously and very quickly the moment you die.

1. Fear

You will find yourself gripped with such gruesome fear, unlike anything you have known before in the world; it is accompanied with utter hopelessness. You will know that you are lost forever and the impending gloom that awaits you.

God allowed me to have such an experience one night in 2002. Suddenly I found myself in a spirit form outside my physical body. I do not know why, but I tried to open the front door of the house we lived in at the time. Each time my hand seemed to slip, miss the latch on the door somehow, and pass right through the door.

After trying desperately for the fourth time to open the front door, I understood that though I had hands, somehow they had lost the ability to feel or even grasp the latch no matter how hard I tried. That frightened me, and I knew that something was terribly wrong. In my helplessness, I cried out to Jesus, wondering why I was in that state.

Much to my relief, Jesus Christ appeared and said to me, "This is what happens to a sinner who dies suddenly without Me. Daughter, I have let you experience this fear and hopelessness that grips the lost sinner. Warn the world not to be unprepared when death strikes."

Reader, it would be very frightening if you die without Jesus Christ in your life, for you will be hopelessly lost. Accepting Jesus Christ provides everlasting consolation and good hope that result in victory, no matter when death strikes. Thanks be to God "who gives us the victory through our Lord Jesus Christ" (1 Cor. 15:57), and "who has loved us and given us everlasting consolation and good hope by grace" (2 Thess. 2:16).

2. Spiritual body

There is a natural body, and there is a spiritual body.

—1 Corinthians 15:44

Death results in a separation of the "real self" from the physical body. The Bible calls this "real self" your spirit, and your spirit continues to exist consciously in spiritual body. Once, you have left your physical body you will have a transparent body. This is your spiritual body that looks like your physical body and has all senses at a much heightened level.

I experienced this as a result of my own close brush with death. The first time, as mentioned in chapter 1, the moment I fell into the rose garden, there was a detachment between my body and self.

I could see my unconscious body lying in the garden, and simultaneously I saw myself safe in the arms of one of the two beautiful angels with wings standing nearby my unconscious body.

Though I was just three and one-half years old at the time, I needed no explanation. Instantly I knew this was the "real me" and the one unconscious was just my body where the real me lived. I also noticed that my senses were much enhanced. For instance, I could see in all directions without the need to turn. Much intrigued by the angel's wings, I touched the edge of the wing to see how it felt; and I also noticed that the sun was much brighter than it normally appeared.

We (the angels and real me) watched as I (my body) was rushed to the hospital. It was all real.

Similarly in the third incident I mentioned in chapter 1, there was a complete detachment between real self and the body. Through the eyes of real self (spirit), I watched my body not breathing and lying still. I saw myself covered with the blanket and also watched my assailant leave. Again, it was all real.

In addition to these incidents, in all my trips to hell, I was separated from my physical body and was present in my spiritual body with all my senses at a much heightened level.

3. Appear naked

A lost sinner appears naked; this symbolizes his or her unrepentant state at the time of death. "Sin is a reproach" (Prov. 14:34) that brings forth shame and everlasting contempt; "and many of those who sleep in the dust of the earth shall awake, Some to everlasting life, Some to shame and everlasting contempt" (Dan. 12:2). Only the blood of Jesus Christ cleanses us from all sin (1 John 1:7) and thereby covers the shame of nakedness that sin brings. "Blessed is he whose transgression is forgiven, Whose sin is covered" (Ps. 32:1).

4. Darkness

A lost sinner sees him or herself in darkness and also sees a path ahead of them engulfed in darkness because their deeds were evil. He or she is naturally inclined to carry on the journey in the path of darkness. At times I also witnessed lost souls compelled on this journey by demons—much against their will and to their doom.

> And this is the condemnation, that the light has come into the world and men loved darkness rather than light, because their deeds were evil. For everyone practicing evil hates the light and does not come to the light, lest his deeds should be exposed.
>
> —JOHN 3:19–20

5. Audience with the Judge

> For it is appointed unto men once to die but after this the judgment.
>
> —HEBREWS 9:27

I witnessed lost souls going through their life reviews and being judged. If these lost souls happened to be escorted by demons at the moment when they went through their life reviews, I noticed that the demons absconded from the scene and reappeared after the judgment was pronounced on the lost soul, to escort them to their doom. In the case of those lost souls unaccompanied by demons on this journey after their life reviews, demons appeared to escort them to hell.

In one such instance, in February 2005, I was instantly translated in my spirit to the courtroom of God and watched the proceedings in session.

For the Father judges no one, but has committed all judgment to the Son.

—JOHN 5:22

For we must all appear before the judgment seat of Christ,
that each one may receive the things done in the body,
according to what he has done, whether good or bad.

—2 CORINTHIANS 5:10

The holy and righteous Jesus Christ in all His fullness was seated
as the judge with a glorious light surrounding Him. The lost soul
stood as a criminal engulfed in darkness. He was once saved and
baptized but had turned away from the truth, had gone back to a
life of perpetual sin, and died unexpectedly. I saw a thick white
book—the Book of Life—in front of Jesus Christ the Judge. I heard
Him say to the lost soul, "Your name is not here."

Fearful of the impending gloom that awaited him, the lost soul
contended the case saying, "I was brought here suddenly." To this,
the Judge replied, "I gave you many chances to repent."

As soon as He uttered those words, I saw an amplified screen
appear and the lost soul's entire life played on this screen from the
time of his birth to the moment he died. I marveled to see each
detail of his life covered. I saw him giving his life to Christ when
he became born again and testifying in water baptism, dedicating
himself for the service of God. I also saw him fall back in sin and
indulge in adultery in his wife's absence. He had thought within
himself that she would never find out those things he had done
behind her back; but he had forgotten that God was watching him.
Everything is naked to the eyes of God (Heb. 4:13).

He will bring every secret thing whether good or bad to
judgment.

—ECCLESIASTES 12:14

Even all his secret thoughts that he thought was known only to him were played back to him. I also watched those chances he was offered in life to repent but had hardened himself. Ashamed and guilty, the lost sinner wept as his life review ended. I watched in amazement as the three witnesses stood up to testify against this lost soul, one by one. The first to testify against him was:

1. The Holy Spirit

The Holy Spirit—through whom this lost soul was once convicted and brought to the saving knowledge of God—appeared as a dove and testified against this lost soul. "No one can say that Jesus is Lord except by the Holy Spirit" (1 Cor. 12:3).

This lost soul had grieved and quenched the Holy Spirit by going back to a life of slavery to sin from which he was once set free and thus had insulted the Spirit of grace. "And do not grieve the Holy Spirit of God, by whom you were sealed for the day of redemption" (Eph. 4:30). "Do not quench the Spirit" (1 Thess. 5:19).

As the one who risked losing his life by breaking the seal of the king, the absolute ultimate authority, similarly this lost soul lost the pledge of security offered by the Holy Spirit by abandoning his Christian walk, "for faith is dead without works" (James 2:26). "Therefore bring fruit worthy of repentance" (Luke 3:8).

Next, I saw the water in which this lost soul was once baptized rise up to testify against him.

2. Water

It was in this water that this lost soul was once baptized, symbolizing his death to sin.

> Therefore we were baptized with Him through baptism into death, that just as Christ was raised from the dead by the glory of the Father, even so we also should walk in newness of life.
> —ROMANS 6:4

Beloved, if you were baptized once and have gone back to the world in a life of sin, this water will rise up against you in which you were baptized.

I, in awe, watched the third witness, the blood of Jesus, testify against this lost soul.

3. Blood

The blood of Jesus rose to testify against him and pressed these two charges:

> a. This lost soul had counted the blood of the covenant by which he was sanctified a common thing.

Of how much worse punishment, do you suppose, will he be thought worthy who has trampled the Son of God underfoot, counted the blood of the covenant by which he was sanctified a common thing, and insulted the Spirit of grace?

—HEBREWS 10:29

> b. Secondly, he had participated unworthily in the Lord's Supper, representing the death and atoning sacrifice of the Son of God, not heeding to the warning in the scripture.

Therefore whoever eats this bread or drinks this cup of the Lord in an unworthy manner will be guilty of the body and blood of the Lord. But let a man examine himself, and so let him eat of the bread and drink of the cup. For he who eats and drinks in an unworthy manner eats and drinks judgment to himself, not discerning the Lord's body. For this reason many are weak and sick among you, and many sleep.

—1 CORINTHIANS 11:27–30

All the three witnesses agreed as one, saying, "He is guilty."

> And there are three that bear witness on earth: the Spirit, the water, and the blood; and these three agree as one.
> —1 John 5:8

I watched as the holy and righteous Judge pronounced His verdict: "Guilty!" to the lost soul. Immensely fearful of the awaiting doom, his pitiful cries filled the courtroom.

> But if anyone draws back, my soul has no pleasure in him.
> —Hebrews 10:38

> But he who does wrong will be repaid for what he has done, and there is no partiality.
> —Colossians 3:25

Make sure on the Day of Judgment you have the three witnesses to testify in your favor so you will have a favorable verdict; if not, you will lose your case before the Judge, Jesus Christ, "who without partiality judges according to each one's work" (1 Pet. 1:17).

This lost soul, while alive, had believed and lived in the deception of the fanciful thinking that once he was saved, it was forever (irrespective of his sinful lifestyle) till his death. He had forgotten that God would hold him accountable for his actions. He had toyed with salvation and viewed it as a license to sin. He had thought no matter what sin he indulged in, he will still make it to heaven minus a few rewards. After his death, he realized that it was a grave error and he was deceived by the enemy.

Beloved, if you are living your life based on this deception, as this lost soul, that once you have been saved it is OK to indulge in sin and will still make it to heaven anyway, you are doomed. Salvation is a gift of God and, therefore, you are indebted to "live for righteousness, having died to sins" (1 Pet. 2:24) being a bond-servant of God (v. 16).

While none of us are perfect and all of us face daily struggles in life, it is our daily commitment to God, offering ourselves at His altar "as a living sacrifice" (Rom. 12:1), and desiring to live by the standard of the Word of God with the help of the Holy Spirit who empowers us that we live victoriously in this sinful world.

There is certainly no excuse to be enslaved again to what we were once freed from after having come to the knowledge of Christ. We cannot continue in perpetual sin and still expect to end up in heaven. "Stand fast therefore in the liberty by which Christ has made us free and do not be entangled again with a yoke of bondage" (Gal. 5:1). "What shall we say then? Shall we continue in sin that grace may abound? Certainly not!" (Rom. 6:1–2).

Do not listen to the lies of the devil and be deceived, for he hates you and wants you to end up in hell. He told Eve, if she ate of the fruit, "You will not surely die" (Gen. 3:4). This was much in contrast to God, who had said, "You shall not eat it, nor shall you touch it, lest you die" (v. 3). Eve, not heeding to God's warning, obeyed the voice of the enemy; that disobedience resulted in serious consequences disastrous to mankind. Also, Adam and Eve were expelled from the Garden of Eden and their fellowship with God was broken. Similarly, if we listen to the voice of the devil and lead a life of disobedience to God's Word in this world while alive, it will result in our eternal separation with God after our death. So heed the voice of God and live: "Work out your own salvation with fear and trembling" (Phil. 2:12).

Beloved, do you consider yourself saved but are living in secret sin? Please repent and renounce your sin, right now.

While God accepts you just as you are when you come to Him for forgiveness of sins, He also expects you to renounce your sin, just as the woman caught in adultery. Jesus said to her, "Go and sin no more" (John 8:11). "Adulterers…will [not] inherit the kingdom of God" (1 Cor. 6:9–10).

While, you are alive, please repent now. If you were to die in your sins, you will be eternally separated from God. Jesus being the "propitiation for our sins, and not for ours only but also for the sins of the whole world" (1 John 2:2) helps us "to obtain mercy and find grace to help in time of need" (Heb. 4:16).

6. Eternal damnation

I beheld lost souls condemned eternally to hell, those who did not have Jesus Christ in their lives as their Lord and Savior. I witnessed those lost souls weep inconsolably for having rejected the salvation plan offered in Jesus Christ freely and thus missed the opportunity to go to heaven.

I also saw those lost souls who had thought that they were saved and also served Him in ministry but ended up in hell where there is "weeping and gnashing of teeth" (Luke 13:28) and "their worm does not die and the fire is not quenched" (Mark 9:48).

7. Angels weep

> There is rejoicing in the presence of angels of God over one sinner who repents.
>
> —LUKE 15:10

Beloved, as angels rejoice over one sinner who repents, they also weep over lost sinners who are on their way to hell.

I witnessed this on two different occasions. The angels of God appeared to be heartbroken and sobbed out loud over these unrepentant sinners about to depart the earth. In both the cases, the souls had been born again at one time but had backslidden and departed from the truth. These angels had waited till the very end for them to repent and come back to God. Aware of the damnation that awaited these lost souls, they wept in sorrow.

Chapter Three

WITNESSING SOULS BEFORE
AND AFTER DEATH

Jesus Christ allowed me to witness many lost souls right before and after their death. I mention a few below.

1. One evening in the year 2001, Jesus appeared to me, took my hand, and asked me to accompany Him. Instantly I found us in another land standing right in front of a small house. I could see a sickly woman who lay inside this house. She was coughing incessantly. Jesus told me to watch carefully and said that she was going to die soon.

As soon as He said those words, I saw two huge demons stand next to her to take her with them. That poor woman became fearful; she could see them, no doubt. She began to shake vigorously in fear and suddenly breathed her last.

The very next moment, I saw her in her spirit body next to where her body lay. She did not want to accompany these demons and put up a stiff resistance. They were much more powerful than she was and subdued her easily. Though she appeared to have a good stature, she was simply no match to their strength. They commanded her to follow them. I heard them say, "We have come to escort you to hell." Then I saw her being dragged on a path of darkness to hell. It appeared that neither the woman nor the demons could see us.

Jesus said sorrowfully, "She rejected My plan of salvation." Saying that, Jesus held my hand and I found myself instantly back at home.

2. In the year 2005 I beheld a lost soul of a man on his way to hell. He had just died in a hospital. At his death he knew what was in store for him, and he was very frightened of his journey ahead. He saw me and pleaded for me to help him. I saw that he was covered in darkness and the path ahead of him was in darkness too. He was forced to carry on his dreadful journey much against his will.

3. In the same year I was instantly translated in my spirit to a hospital and watched a man right before his death. I beheld two demons of short stature sit on his chest. Instantly he suffered a massive heart attack that resulted in his death. After he died I saw him in a spirit form that put up a fight with these demons. No matter how much he fought with them, though he seemed to have a good stature, he was no match for their strength and was soon overpowered and escorted to hell by these same demons.

4. In the year 2007 again I was instantly translated in my spirit to a hospital and beheld a young man breathe his last. The very moment he closed his eyes in this world, I saw him in spirit form next to his body crying hopelessly, saying, "I had many dreams." He was lamenting over his death since he had died young without having realized any of his dreams. I could see that he was covered in darkness and knew what lay ahead of him that added to his sorrow.

5. In the year 2008, I was taken by Jesus Christ to a faraway country and found us standing next to a railway crossing. Jesus asked me to watch carefully. I could see a man who appeared to be drunk trying to cross the railway track. In his inebriated state he failed to notice the fast approaching train; and as a result, he was run over by the train and killed instantly. The very next moment I saw him in his spirit form standing next to his body. He appeared to be fearful. He looked at himself and lamented, "Oh, God! What happened? I killed myself." He was in all his senses, completely

sober, and aware of what had happened to him. Though the body was dead, his spirit was very much alive. I could see him covered in darkness and a dark path that lay ahead of him.

6. One late night in 2009, I was instantly translated in my spirit to a well-known personality's bedroom. I saw him die and watched as he stood outside his body in a spirit form. I could see him covered in darkness. He appeared to be lost with his death as he looked at his physical body in disbelief; he had not expected to die so soon. He even attempted to get back in his physical body in desperation. As he tried to do so, the two demons who had come to escort him to hell laughed at him. I watched him wail and lament when he realized that it was impossible to enter back into his physical body. As he looked at his physical body, I heard him say repeatedly with regret, "What have I done?" I saw as those demons dragged and forced him on a path ahead of him covered in darkness.

7. In the year 2010 I beheld a lost soul of a woman. She was a preacher's wife. She was dressed in a dirty torn garment that was once a white robe. While alive, she, along with her husband, had demanded gold and silver in the name of the Lord for His work. But instead they had used it on themselves. Soon after, she died of a wasting disease.

I saw her plead with God to let her in heaven. I heard the voice of the Lord say, "Depart from Me, ye wicked; I do not know you." She wept inconsolably as demons dragged her to hell.

Ministers of God, please do not rob God's money. You might be used of God today; but if you are robbing what belongs to God, you will find yourself in hell.

> Many will say to Me in that day, "Lord, Lord, have we not prophesied in Your name, cast out demons in Your name, and done many wonders in Your name?" And then I will

declare to them, "I never knew you; depart from Me, you
who practice lawlessness!"

—MATTHEW 7:22–23

8. In the year 2011 I was instantly translated to a place where
a young man was involved in sexually perverse activities. I could
see two demons; one on each side of this young man. I saw them
encourage him to go ahead with this act of perversion. They did so
by whispering in his ears. He was not aware of their presence and
mistook their whispers as his own thoughts. Attempting an eroge-
nous asphyxiation, he tied a noose around his neck, which resulted
in his accidental death. With his death he stood in his spirit form
next to his body in darkness and now was able to see those demons.

He had mistaken their whispers in his ears as his own thoughts
and killed himself. He appeared to be very fearful of these demons
and wailed as they grabbed him. I could see him forced along the
path covered in darkness as they escorted him to his doom.

Has the devil been whispering in your ears to involve yourself
in immoral activities? Beware; do not pay heed to them. If you
are involved in such activities, please repent and be saved in Jesus'
name. If you were to die in this state, as the mentioned soul, you
will end up in hell. God is holy and wants you to be holy. "Now the
body is not for sexual immorality but for the Lord, and the Lord for
the body" (1 Cor. 6:13).

9. In the year 2012 I beheld a gang of lost souls of murderers. They
had all been shot dead. I saw them all covered in darkness. They
appeared extremely fearful of the many demons that surrounded
them. I saw them all wail and lament as they were forced by those
demons to continue their journey engulfed in darkness. They all
knew that they were lost.

10. In the same year I witnessed yet another soul who had just
died. Her grandson was with her at the moment of her passing. I

saw her in spirit form right next to where her body lay. I could see that she was in darkness and a dark path lay ahead of her. Before he left to make funeral arrangements, I heard her grandson utter, "Rest in peace, Nan." With that, tears streamed down her face. She was frightened of what lay ahead of her; and she also knew that, contrary to the belief of her grandson, she would never be able to rest in peace.

Chapter Four

ABOUT HELL

To enter the abode of the damned was an experience in itself. It was to plunge myself in the dark kingdom of death and be surrounded by the sheer horror of the continual torment accompanied with the miserable cries of eternal regret of those imprisoned there and for whom there is no escape.

Each time I was instantly translated in my spirit to hell and was present there in my spirit form. I found my senses at a much heightened level. I saw and felt the ground on which we walked. Jesus held my hand most of the times and helped me walk as I entered those places which otherwise would have been humanly impossible. He also explained those things there which otherwise would have been impossible for me to ever know and understand.

I noticed each part of hell was significantly different than the rest. I also saw fire in hell and experienced the scorching heat of the place that is unlike anything in this world; it resulted in leaving me parched with an excessive desire for water. I found the putrid smell of burning flesh and brimstone absolutely revolting. I witnessed the acute ghastly torture meted out to the condemned. The lost souls felt every horrible torture inflicted to them. As I watched the lost in their miserable state, I understood why Jesus Himself warned many times about hell and not to go there.

During these experiences I realized that sometimes Jesus alone was visible, at times both of us were visible, and there were also times when neither of us was visible. Also, the conversations that Jesus and I had with the lost souls seemed to be unheard by the demons. Through the light of Jesus I was able to see and perceive things in that place of darkness, but at times we also came across dimly lit lanterns.

Hell is very literal as mentioned in the Bible. I found that in hell there was a reason behind everything that appeared there. It could only be discerned spiritually, not logically through human wisdom but in the light of God and His Word. Logical discernment fails and results in limitation of the wisdom of God.

> But the natural man does not receive the things of the Spirit of God, for they are foolishness to him; nor can he know them, because they are spiritually discerned.
> —1 CORINTHIANS 2:14

Hell enlarges itself.

> Therefore Sheol has enlarged itself And opened its mouth beyond measure; Their glory and their multitude and their pomp, And he who is jubilant, shall descend into it.
> —ISAIAH 5:14

And I witnessed this as a fact. Twice I saw a heavy equipment vehicle there, unlike anything I have seen in this world, which emitted no sound at all and was used for that very purpose. Apart from the many other things that I saw there, I also saw coals. The hours that I spent there appeared as a matter of minutes.

I witnessed lost souls from the enormously wealthy, well-known eminent personalities, and intellectuals—all well respected while on earth—to the ordinary. Death comes to all whether rich, not rich, or poor. One day, in spite of your wealth, power, riches, fame, etc., you will stand in the presence of the Creator of the universe to face the judgment. Make sure on that day, whenever that might be, you have a clean slate.

I noticed the two significant reasons common to all lost souls in hell:

1. Sin

> For the wages of sin is death.
>
> —ROMANS 6:23

I saw huge blots on these lost souls and wondered what they meant. Jesus, reading my thoughts, answered, "Their sins appear as blots; the reward of their unrighteousness."

While on earth they got away with all their secret sins known only to them. But after their death and entrance to hell, all the sins they had reveled in while alive were visible unto all. They were now ashamed of their deeds.

> For nothing is secret, that shall not be made manifest; neither any thing hid, that shall not be known and come abroad.
>
> —LUKE 8:17, KJV

Jesus, with immense sorrow, said, "If only they had asked Me while alive to wash their sins! I would have done so and remembered their sins no more. Now it is too late."

Jesus asked me to look closely at those stains. To my amazement, each sin committed by the lost soul while alive was written in bold black letters. In hell the lost soul was identified by the sins he or she had committed on earth.

The sins appeared like these (as shown in the picture on the left) on their forms.

> Nothing in all creation is hidden from God's sight. Everything is uncovered and laid bare before the eyes of him to whom we must give account.
> —Hebrews 4:13, niv

Sin results in eternal separation from God. If you lead your life on earth away from God, after your death you will reap this. If you draw near to God, He will draw near to you (James 4:8). But if you move away from God on earth, after your death this is what you will receive: an eternal separation from God.

2. Rejection of the Savior Jesus Christ

In death the lost souls know automatically that they missed accepting Jesus Christ as their Savior who alone could have saved them from hell since He is the only way, truth, and life (John 14:6). I never witnessed even one lost soul being explained this fact.

The crux of the matter is that if you refuse to accept Jesus as the way, the truth, and the life while alive in this world, you will do so after death. And then it will be too late. Please do not take this lightly; it's a question of eternity. Make a decision to accept Jesus now.

I beheld lost souls utterly remorseful and cursing themselves. In some cases these lost souls even cursed the particular person who could have given them the gospel of Jesus Christ but did not do so. So, if you are saved, please do not contain this good news to yourself; share it with others too! I heard these lost souls say, "Why did he or she who knew me not tell me about Jesus?" They all lamented missing the opportunities they had on earth to receive the forgiveness of sins offered freely in Jesus Christ. The following are some of the statements I heard over and over again:

- "If only I had accepted Jesus, I would not be here today."

- "I knew about Jesus, but I did not know that it was this serious."

- "Why did I not listen to that man or woman who shared with me about Jesus?"

- "I thought Jesus was *one* of the ways."

- "I did not think I will end up in hell; now I am lost forever."

I noticed that these lost souls in hell had believed sincerely one of the following while alive:

a. Some had believed that their existence would cease after death.

b. Some had believed that they would be reincarnated.

c. Some were unprepared for death as a result of sudden death—murdered, accidents, etc. They had thought that they had time on their side but death struck them unexpectedly.

d. Some of the lost souls were in hell because they had believed that Jesus Christ was *one* of the ways to God, not the *only* way. Their beliefs were contrary to what the Bible teaches about Jesus Christ

Nor is there salvation in any other, for there is no other name under heaven given among men by which we must be saved.

—Acts 4:12

e. Some had expected to end up in heaven but were shocked to end up in hell. That included the following two categories:

1. Those who had believed that they were good people hence deserved heaven.

2. Those who believed that once they were saved it was forever and had indulged in all sorts of sins.

You might consider yourself to be a good person, but you need to make a personal decision for Jesus Christ. The Bible says, "All have sinned and fall short of the glory of God" (Rom. 3:23). God does not condone sin. It is so serious that it results in death. Jesus Christ had to take our place and die on the cross for our sins and redeem us by His blood. Salvation cannot be earned through good works: "not of works, lest anyone should boast" (Eph. 2:9). In humility acknowledge that you are a sinner and receive Jesus as your Savior.

Those that believed they were saved forever thought that no matter what they did with their lives, after death God would receive them in heaven anyway. After their death these lost souls realized that they were deceived by the enemy. I saw many such lost souls in hell.

Beloved, once you are saved, God expects you not to be entangled in the bondage of sin again; for in doing so, you make yourself an enemy of the cross of Christ. "For many walk, of whom I have told you often, and now tell you even weeping, that they are the enemies of the cross of Christ" (Phil. 3:18).

f. Some believed God does not send anyone to hell.

The Bible says that hell was "prepared for the devil and his angels" (Matt. 25:41). If you reject God's salvation plan, you are condemned to hell. God has made a provision for us in Jesus Christ His Son to escape hell. Jesus warned about hell, not to go there.

> If your hand causes you to sin, cut it off. It is better for you
> to enter into life maimed, rather than having two hands, to
> go to hell, into the fire that shall never be quenched—where
> "Their worm does not die And the fire is not quenched."
> —MARK 9:43–44

> But the cowardly, unbelieving, abominable, murderers, sex-
> ually immoral, sorcerers, idolaters, and all liars shall have
> their part in the lake which burns with fire and brimstone,
> which is the second death.
> —REVELATION 21:8

Jesus wept as He said to me, "If only they had asked Me while alive to wash their sins, they would not be here today. They chose to live a willful life of separation from Me while on earth, so they have received what they wanted—an eternal separation from Me after death. It was their decision."

The consequences of their rejection of salvation offered freely in Jesus Christ resulted in the following:

1. Eternal damnation

They knew that they are doomed forever; there is no escape, no way out ever.

2. Degree of torment

Each soul received the degree of torment in accordance to his or her sins. I saw that their sins were embedded in their forms and stood out.

> But he who does wrong will be repaid for what he has done,
> and there is no partiality.
> —COLOSSIANS 3:25

> Do not be deceived, God is not mocked; for whatever a
> man sows, that he will also reap.
> —GALATIANS 6:7

3. Continual torment

I witnessed lost souls subjected to cruel continual torment by these ugly, hideous, fearsome demons who were specially assigned to inflict those tortures on them. I saw the demons derive sadistic pleasures while carrying out those torments. This cycle was non-stop. In spite of the mournful cries, wailings, and pleadings of those condemned, there was no mercy, no respite. Some souls asked for death while their tormentors laughed sarcastically and said, "This is your death." Lost souls appeared absolutely helpless in front of these vicious demons.

4. Age and appearance

Their spirit bodies were just in the shape of their physical bodies. Looking at them, I could tell instantly whether it was a male or a female. Also, they appeared to be the same age as at the time of their death; and whether the cause of their death was by accident, disease, murder, etc., it was clearly apparent on their forms and on the exact spot. I beheld a lost soul with a deep scar in his neck. Jesus told me that he had hung himself.

5. Knowledge of who among their loved ones would end up in hell

The lost souls know and are concerned about their loved ones who will end up there unless they repent. I witnessed the condemned cry out saying so and even begged me to warn their families not to come there. I heard a lost soul of a man cry out, "My wife will come here."

Just like in the parable of the rich man, we see that he was concerned and knew his brothers would end up there unless they repented.

> Then he said, "I beg you therefore, father, that you would send him to my father's house, for I have five brothers, that

he may testify to them, lest they also come to this place of torment."

—LUKE 16:27–28

6. No family reunions

Apart from the agony of the torment, the lost souls never get to see the ones they had loved so much on earth.

I never saw any babies or little children in hell. Jesus told me that any person with developmental disabilities since their birth and not able to understand salvation were not found in hell.

Chapter Five

DEMONS IN HELL

I FOUND HELL TO be a very busy place and extremely well guarded by the innumerable demons who keep the imprisoned souls from escaping. These demons emit foul odors from their forms and are fearsome, spiteful beings with weird features. I saw some with animal-like bodies; for example, crocodile-like tails, bat-like ears and wings, and tongues swishing like serpents.

The Bible mentions that Satan chose to rebel against God and one-third of the angels joined his army to oppose God. As a result of that rebellion, God cast them down to earth.

Though hell has been prepared for the devil and his demons, as mentioned in Matthew 25:41, they have not yet been consigned to their ultimate fate of punishment in the lake of fire. It is only after the final judgment that they will be cast into the lake of fire where they will be tormented day and night forever and ever (Rev. 20:10).

Satan's army of one-third of the angels who rebelled with him, he has assigned to certain territories, geographical locations, nations, etc. And there are also demons assigned in hell to carry out certain tasks. The role of demons is best understood as torturers.

In Matthew 18:23–34 is a parable of the master who was angry with his unrepentant, wicked servant and eventually delivered him to the torturers as a punishment. Jesus, while sharing this parable, made it clear that a similar punishment awaited all those who sinned (v. 35). In this parable the sin mentioned is unforgiveness. However, the punishment is not only restricted to unforgiveness; it can be applied to any other sin.

I witnessed these evil beings inflict gruesome tortures, terrorize the lost souls, and also derive sadistic pleasures while meting out these cruel acts. I saw that there was a great anticipation and a sense of achievement and rejoicing in hell whenever a soul arrived there. I heard these demons say to each other with glee, "Another one! Another one!"

Satan is a hard taskmaster and demons are meant to perform. In addition to their immense hatred for God and mankind, they had a fear of Satan. I saw them work very hard to get more souls to hell; otherwise Satan punished them. There were ranks among them, and they appeared to work in perfect coordination. I also witnessed the lower ranked demons fight each other and work in subjection to the ones who exercised authority over them.

These demons also escort those souls who are condemned to hell. At times, right before his or her death, an unsaved person sees these demons that are sent to escort him or her to hell. In view of this, these lost souls also make certain statements filled with obvious fear of the terror that lies ahead and put up a struggle in an effort not to accompany the demons.

I witnessed many such souls before their death as their spirit eyes opened. Irrespective of the fact that they lived their lives far away from God in sin, yet they were able to view these demons that had come to escort them to hell. Being face-to-face with the sheer reality of the horror that awaited them, they put up a stiff resistance to these ugly, evil beings—a reflection of their terror-filled future. This stark reality faced by a lost soul prior to his or her death is often dismissed as hallucinations.

If you happen to be one such person undergoing these experiences and are fearful as a result, please repent and be saved right now in Jesus' name. Once you are washed in the blood of Jesus, these demons will flee from you.

These demons do not approach a person about to die to escort them to hell by chance. Your sin identifies you with them. Your life on earth is watched closely by God and also by Satan. If you happen to leave the world in an unrepentant state, this fact is neither hidden from God or from Satan, who sends these demons to fetch a person once it is time to leave the earth. I also saw lost souls travel on their doomed journey to hell at times unaccompanied by demons up to a certain point after which they were joined by demons who escorted them to hell. You must know that Satan knows those who belong to him and therefore sends these demons to escort them to their damnation in hell.

Reader, if you are leading a double life in this world, portraying a godly image on the outside while reveling in secret sins, you are fooling nobody other than yourself. Neither God nor Satan can be fooled by your portrayed outside image. It is your inside that actually matters whether you are living a righteous life in Christ or practicing a life governed by sin. Your judgment that takes you either to heaven or hell is based on this fact.

I also noticed that after escorting the condemned to hell, these demons also reported this to those in charge over them. Thus via prompt reporting through his network of demons, Satan is kept well informed of all the activities within his control.

Apart from the various tasks they perform, I saw those demons dig pits and prepare the cells for the lost souls about to die and enter hell. I also saw them stoke up fires within the pits to keep them hot.

I found that even demons do not like to be found in hell, which has been created for them and Satan. Hence, they prefer to be found on earth, as one would prefer to chill out in cool places in summer; in any case, no summer can ever be compared to the heat of hell. Hence, they wait earnestly to be dispatched from hell. Once on earth, they carry out the bidding of Satan with the help of many other demons already in the world. Unsuccessful missions always result in discipline and a warning to be sent back to hell. I noticed that successful completion of an assignment was acknowledged with heinous laughter and a promise of reward while a failed assignment resulted in instant severe discipline. I witnessed a lower rank demon being hit and yelled at by the demon in charge over him for failing to successfully complete the given assignment.

These demons, once on earth, do everything to stay here and inhabit places—those they share an affinity and allegiance with and opened already to them. They also are on a constant look out for new territories. Haunted grounds can be cited as a most common example of where these demons throng in large numbers.

These demons can also inhabit those human beings who open themselves to them in any form. At times these demons prompt unbiblical and ungodly principles within these individuals they inhabit and use them to promote them as new concepts. These new concepts presented in an attractive layout, spread like wildfire and gain huge popularity. These ungodly concepts become an instant hit and a great success. In the process they ensnare many through their appeal and charm. If given room in a life, they will lead one far away from the one true God.

Christians, be on guard against such unbiblical concepts that spring up suddenly and quickly gain worldwide publicity. These ideas are not coincidental but implanted by the enemy on purpose to lead many to sin and fall away from the truth. Meanwhile, the person inhabited by the demon is deceived into believing the idea as her or his own.

I beheld one such lost soul. As soon as this once well-known woman died, I saw, much to my shock, a powerful demon slip out of her just as one would slip out of his or her clothing. I could see that she was unaware of her possession by this demon and appeared shell shocked to see it slip out of her.

This demon had led her to promote sexual immorality on a large scale leading many to sin. She was deceived into believing that concept was her own; and it had given her worldwide publicity. It was only with her death that she realized that she was deceived by the enemy.

This demon that inhabited her also escorted her to hell. I saw him being congratulated by none other than Satan himself, who said to him, "Well done." After this I saw this demon immediately leave for earth, ready to take on his next assignment.

Demons hate God and His creation—mankind—and work for the destruction of them. These extremely wicked beings are Satan's army. Apart from the many evil things they are engaged in, I also heard them blaspheme God with utter profanities similar to what I have heard in the world. I could see a connection between them and the sins that are prevalent in the world. I saw that the wickedness so rampant in this world comes from Satan and his demons. The obscenities we hear on earth are an imprint of the original that I heard in hell. It is no wonder that in this world all vulgar cursing and swearing is directed only at Jesus Christ the Savior and no other worshipped deity.

The Word of God directs us that no perverse conversation should come forth of our lips: "Put perverse lips far from you" (Prov. 4:24).

Beloved, if you open yourself to sin, you soon become a slave to that sin. To curse and swear and mouth obscenities is an attribute of Satan. Please repent if you have been sinning in this area and pledge not to participate in this again.

These demons are very deceptive. I have seen them change their forms to animals, men or women, beings of light, and even take the form of children. Reader, has something been appearing to you? You need to know that not every angel that might manifest is of God. While the angel of God makes one to focus on God, the counterfeit angel removes one's focus from God to self-worship. Beware of these deceptive evil spirits who seek to remove your focus from the Savior Jesus Christ to themselves.

Satan and his demons can take any form and love to be worshipped. No matter how loving they may appear on the outside, it is only a deception to get you under their control. In reality they hate you and seek to destroy you. Hence, do not give them any place. Resist them in Jesus' name and they will flee from you (James 4:7).

Chapter Six

A WARNING FOR THE FUTURE

1995

A s a result of my born-again experience in the year 1993, Jesus became my first love. This was an important chapter that gave my life a newfound meaning, and I was never the same again. He was the center of my being, and I was committed to do His will. The day Jesus became my first love, He became very real to me. This love affair with Jesus turned serious, and the time that I spent in His presence stretched from minutes to hours as months passed by.

Earlier I had struggled to read the Bible; and when I succeeded in my attempt to do so, I found it boring. My view of God was that of a dictator who controlled us, the helpless and mortal beings who were but mere puppets in His hands. We were resigned to our fate under His dictatorship.

Thank God everything changed with my conversion. God of my imagination had proven to be different from God in reality. I yearned for a living relationship with Him and began to seek Him earnestly—desiring and seeking deeper truths of the Word of God.

I was enraptured by His love. The deep love of Jesus beckoned me to drink from His river, the river of life, and I valued that sweet fellowship with my Savior when my spirit was tuned to His. I found that purely ecstatic, and I began to look forward to these times.

One weekend in 1995 I decided to spend the day in prayer. Whenever I was alone I loved to pray, forgetting the outside world. I cherished these precious moments of spiritual rendezvous with God.

It was 10:30 in the morning and I was down on my knees offering sacrifices of praise. Suddenly somebody called out my name. The voice sounded familiar, and I opened my eyes and looked up. And what I saw will forever remain engraved in my memory.

With naked eyes I saw Jesus walk through the door in a glistening white robe. I recognized His voice that spoke to me every day, taught me His Word, and guided me on the path I was to go. Today was the first time I was seeing Him in person. He was real.

Every part of my being cried out, "Jesus! Jesus!" There was a brilliant aura of radiance around Him, and I was completely caught up with His magnetic personality. Those eyes that looked at me were the most piercing I had ever seen, and they seemed to read my heart.

I trembled in awe as I beheld Jesus in His majesty. As He walked toward me, my attention shifted from His eyes to His nail-pierced feet. He stood in front of me and said, "I am Jesus of Nazareth," and stretched His nail-pierced hands toward me.

Trembling, I looked at Him with eagerness and was overwhelmed with happiness. His eyes shone as He went on to say, "My daughter, from now on I will appear to you and also take you to many parts of hell and heaven. You must share this with the people of the world. They must know that the keys of hell have been given to *Me*. I am the way, the truth, and the life."

Jesus then touched my eyes. Immediately I was transported to the days of Noah. I stood with Jesus as a bystander. I could see Noah building the ark. It looked as if his heart was into completing this task given of God.

I saw passersby as they scourged bitter comments at Noah, called him a maniac, and laughed at him; but Noah, unscathed by the comments, continued building the ark.

At last, the ark was completed and he started to take all kinds of birds and animals inside that ark. Some of the species were breathtakingly beautiful as I saw them for the first time in my life. Suddenly I saw the door of the ark being closed, and I could see the water appear everywhere. The level of the water rose to a tremendous height, and Noah's ark started to float on the water.

I saw those passersby who had mocked and laughed at Noah drown in the water and cry for help as they struggled for life. Alas, it was too late and their cries died down. I saw their bodies float in the water. This scene was heartrending.

Jesus then began to speak, "When My gospel is proclaimed to the people, they refuse to accept its reality and Me as their Savior. Just as when Noah was building the ark and getting prepared for the floods that awaited them, in disbelief people refused to accept the reality of floods and the need of the ark to save their lives. They cried out for help when it was too late. In the same manner the people in the present time ridicule and mock My salvation plan, but they cry out for help when it is too late. They are lost, lost forever. These people enter into eternal condemnation and separation to hell. There is hope only while they are alive. If they accept Me as their Savior, I will wash all their sins away and they will not have to go to hell. Every person who is stubborn and refuses to acknowledge Me as their Savior while living will find their place in hell. Go, warn the people; tell them 'I am the way, the truth, and the life. No one comes to the Father except through Me' (John 14:6); and he who has Me has life (1 John 5:12)."

As soon as Jesus finished speaking those words, I saw in front of me a bomb placed inside a rocket. It was only a few seconds and I heard a loud thud. There was a powerful explosion that resulted in a massive destruction. I saw piles of bodies thrown in all directions and blood splattered everywhere.

The words of Jesus echoed in my ears, "This is a warning for the future. Go warn the people, especially the young. For the end will come when they least expect it. Let them not be allured by the various traps of sin; instead let them give themselves to Me. If they confess their sins, I will forgive and receive them. Tell them, My daughter, that I am *the* Way, not *a* way." Saying thus, Jesus disappeared.

Still shaken from the entire episode, I turned to look at the time on the table clock. It was half past eleven. An exact hour had passed since I had knelt in prayer, yet it seemed like a matter of minutes. This was all unbelievable yet true. It was a warning for the future, and I silently resolved to let the world know and be warned.

My dear readers, please do not miss this opportunity to come to Jesus; for the time is too short, life is uncertain, and death is nearer than it appears.

Chapter Seven

A GLIMPSE OF HELL

1995

MY EARLIER ENCOUNTER with Jesus resulted in the addition of a new dimension in my relationship with Him. Now I searched the Scripture with much more eagerness and enthusiasm and my prayer times lengthened.

Few weeks had passed since the warning for the future. Home early from the university, I decided to make use of this opportunity by spending time in prayer. I looked for opportunities to be alone with the Creator to seek and know Him. He was my life, and I needed Him to survive.

In the midst of worship, I saw Him. There He was; my master, Jesus Christ. My room was illuminated with His glory. I was lost looking at His illumined countenance, and then He smiled the most beautiful and captivating smile.

He came near me, held my hand, and said, "My daughter, come with Me." As soon as He uttered those words, I instantly found us near a dark tunnel.

Jesus said, "Watch. This is the entrance of hell." I could see a dim yellow light above this tunnel. I could see that the tunnel was bustling with activity though it was in darkness. There were many ugly demons inside the tunnel. I also saw scores of young men and women enter this tunnel and become overpowered by these demons that waited inside to receive them. Upon seeing these demons, the souls attempted to run back but to no avail; they were all caught by the demons.

These souls helplessly struggled to free themselves but were no match to these demonic brutes in terms of their strength and size. I could hear their helpless pitiful cries. As I continued to watch in horror, I could see that the tunnel led to a pathway that seemed to be full of pits raging with huge flames of fire. I saw those demons throw each of those helpless beings into those pits of fire. Their heartrending cries and screams filled the place.

Just then Jesus began to speak, "These lost souls that you just witnessed among them are many who overdosed and a few who died in gang fights. They all wasted their lives in worldly pleasures and died in sin." Jesus spoke these words with immense sorrow. He went on to say, "Now there is no hope for these souls. There is only hope as long as one is alive; but after death, it is too late. They are lost forever."

I looked at the ground where we stood, it appeared to be burned and made of ash. Strong nauseous stench of burning flesh filled the smoky air.

The dead who were cast into their eternal doom were much alive and seemed to experience everything that was happening to them. I could see that they wanted out of the place, but those demons, who seemed to be assigned to them, intently watched over each of them. Any attempts to get out of the fire resulted in being pushed deeper into the fire.

Their cries and helplessness moved me to tears. Their desperate cries echoed in my ears, and I wanted so much to help them. Jesus spoke again, "Go warn the young people. Tell them not to be lost in the worthless pleasures of the world, for it kills them in the end. They are trading their souls for these pleasures, which are traps laid by the devil to take them to hell."

Jesus took my hand and said, "What you have seen is a glimpse of hell. I will show you much more." With that, I instantly found myself back in the room.

Rejoice, O young man, in your youth, And let your heart cheer you in the days of your youth; Walk in the ways of your heart, And in the sight of your eyes; But know that for all these God will bring you into judgment....Remember now your Creator in the days of your youth, Before the difficult days come, And the years draw near when you say, "I have no pleasure in them."

—ECCLESIASTES 11:9, 12:1

Chapter Eight

A DARK TUNNEL

IN 2008 SUDDENLY Jesus Christ appeared to me, held my hand, and asked me to follow Him. As soon as He said those words, I found us instantly in front of the dark tunnel. I recognized this tunnel as I had seen it earlier (mentioned in the last chapter) as the entrance of hell.

I saw a group of souls standing close to the tunnel. This group was comprised of men and women of all age groups and races. They seemed to be staring right ahead, each lost in herself or himself, and appeared oblivious of others. I saw demons watch them earnestly from inside the tunnel and wait in anticipation for them to enter the tunnel. It looked to me that these demons were specifically assigned to them.

Jesus explained to me saying, "These are people who are fighting between life and death. Some of them have overdosed and some of them have attempted suicide. They are not dead yet. Some of them regret what they have done. Even if they repent at this stage, I will forgive them."

As Jesus spoke these words, I saw a young man approach the tunnel. Jesus told me that he had attempted to kill himself. This young man came and stood near the tunnel, and he appeared to see Jesus. He began to cry out aloud, saying, "What I have done is sin! Jesus, please forgive me! I do not want to go into that darkness! Give me a chance!"

As soon as he said that, I watched as Jesus walked toward this young man and embraced him with much compassion and wiped his tears. I was touched to see the father heart of God. Jesus spoke words of comfort to this young man as He wiped his tears. I heard Him say, "I am giving you another chance." The moment Jesus spoke those words, I saw this young man return back. Jesus looked at me and said, "He will live."

With that, He took my hand and said, "Come with Me." Instantly I found us in an unknown place and standing on a large strip of land. I saw paramedics work on that young man's bloodied body. I heard one of them say, "We are too late. His car was a wreck." Suddenly the young man opened his eyes. I saw the same paramedic ecstatically exclaim, "He is alive! I thought we had lost him!"

Dear reader, please do not experiment with your life. I have seen this dark tunnel, the entrance of hell that leads to fiery pits raging with huge flames of fire. Those fiery pits have been especially prepared and kept for lost souls. I have seen demons throw lost souls into these pits where their torment never ends.

No matter how far you may have strayed away from God and how lost you may be today, Jesus has come to seek you and wants to save you. Please do not reject Him. Give all your burdens and worries to Him, for there is nothing too difficult for Him. Whatever your burden or cause of your problem, Jesus will take care of it. "Come to Me, all you who are weary and burdened, and I will give you rest" (Matt. 11:28, NIV).

In July 2012 I was instantly translated in the spirit and found Jesus and me standing in front of this dark tunnel again. Jesus said to me, "Daughter, today I will take you inside this tunnel and show you what happens there."

He held my hand and we began to walk right inside the tunnel. Though there was a dim light outside the tunnel, the tunnel in itself was in pitch darkness. Through the light of Jesus I could see screeching bats, slithering serpents, and hordes of ugly demonic beings inside this tunnel. Some of the demons seemed to be waiting in glee to escort the lost to their doom while some of them appeared to be complaining, restless, and mouthing profanities while they waited. I heard one say, "How long?" Jesus told me these are waiting to be dispatched to earth.

We came almost to the rear end of the tunnel and stood there. Jesus asked me to watch carefully. I saw two powerful demons posted there. They did not seem to notice us. Right at that moment I saw Satan enter the tunnel with a host of demons surrounding him. He also did not seem to notice us. He stopped there, and I heard him commend these two demons for what a wonderful job they were doing for him and promised he would reward them suitably. He also instructed and urged them to keep doing the work with the same efficiency.

At that moment, I saw a soul come at a lightning speed and stop right at the rear end of the tunnel. Right in front of my eyes, I saw Satan transform himself to Buddha and appear to this soul. I heard him speak soothing words of recovery to this soul.

After a while, I saw this soul go back. Right after this soul had gone back, I saw yet another soul come at a lightning speed and stop. Again, Satan transformed himself instantly; this time it was to a loving being of light that appeared welcoming and non-condemning, and again spoke words of comfort as he had spoken to the previous soul that you will be fine, not to worry. After a while this soul also went back.

I marveled to see his transformation that had happened instantly, one to Buddha and another to loving being of light. He had deceived both these souls into believing that they had actually met the person in accordance to their faith. After these souls went back, I heard Satan laugh. He had tricked them into believing that whatever they had seen and met was the truth. I heard him say, "These are mine; these are mine," in reference to the souls that had gone back.

He instructed those two demons to continue doing the same work with efficiency and left in a hurry to earth. Jesus told me that these two demons were placed here for that very purpose, to deceive people.

With that, Jesus asked me to watch carefully. As He said this, I saw another soul come at a lightning speed and stop. I saw one of the demons appear to this soul instantly in the form of Mary and spoke the same comforting words of recovery; then I saw this soul go back. He had enacted the deception with exact perfection, just like his master. I saw yet another soul come and stop; this time the other demon transformed instantly in the form of Shiva (god of destruction) and spoke words of comfort. I saw this soul also go back. After these souls had returned back, I saw these two demons congratulate each other for fooling the poor souls.

Jesus told me that these souls that I had just seen come at lightning speed and go back were the souls of people who were in life-threatening situations but would recover from their ailments and not die yet.

Satan and his demons deceive such souls who belong to him by manifesting in front of them in the form revered and worshipped by these souls and also by speaking false words of recovery knowing all along they would recover anyway.

These souls were falsely led to believe that they actually encountered the deity they worshipped and also recovered from a death-like situation because of that deity. As a result, not only will these souls continue to be deceived but they will also refute the truth that contrasts their beliefs they strongly hold on to. Satan has been deceiving gullible souls in like manner for a very long time.

Beloved, Satan is a master of deception. I saw that firsthand. I saw him instantly take the form of Buddha and a loving being of light. I also saw his demons transform themselves to Mary and Shiva. Satan and his demons are seriously involved in the business of deceiving ignorant and gullible souls. These demons are actually posted there to deceive men and women of every race day and night. Their purpose is to take them to hell. I heard Satan say, "These are mine," in regard to these souls.

Readers, you need to understand that Satan is a liar and loves to be worshipped in whatever form. "And no wonder! For Satan himself transforms himself into an angel of light" (2 Cor. 11:14).

Jesus is the only way to heaven. Do not be deceived into believing that there is some other way. You are on your way to hell if you believe this. For there is no other way; I have seen it myself. "There is no other name under heaven given among men by which we must be saved" (Acts 4:12) other than the name of Jesus.

Accept Jesus Christ as your Savior today; "now is the day of salvation" (2 Cor. 6:2).

Chapter Nine

MOUTH OF HELL

ONE NIGHT IN May 2009, I was instantly translated in the spirit and found myself standing next to Jesus in a part of hell. We were standing near what appeared to be a well. I found it terribly hot there. I could even feel the heat coming from within the ground I stood on. I noticed the earth where we stood was fragmented and parched due to the intense heat. I felt excessively thirsty just standing there. I was astonished to see a bare blackened tree by the mouth of the well, given the heat of the place and a few black snakes that slithered near its mouth. I also saw two demons waiting outside the well. These demons seemed to be on guard. Neither Jesus nor I appeared to be visible to these demons.

Suddenly Jesus asked me to look into what seemed to be a well. As I looked into this well, I could see that it was dry and immeasurably deep, and apparently was glowing red from deep within. I could not see its bottom. The scorching heat coming from deep within the well hit against my face and left a sharp burning sensation. I felt I was getting burned just by looking at it. I turned my face away quickly, for I could not bear to look into this well.

Then Jesus told me what I had looked into was the abyss. I understood now why the demons had begged Jesus not to send them there before the destined time as mentioned in Luke 8:31: "And they [demons] begged Him that He would not command them to go out into the abyss."

Jesus then asked me to look closely at the mouth of the well. I could see that the well was carved out of rock and it was also possible to seal its mouth.

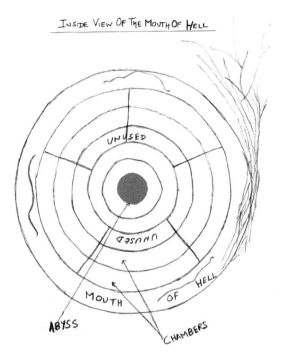

This is an illustration of the mouth of hell. It is much deeper than shown in the picture.

Chapter Ten

CHAMBERS IN HELL

UDDENLY JESUS SAID, "Daughter, we are going inside that place." With that, I instantly found us right underneath the mouth of the well. It was humanly impossible to get into that place without Jesus. There was no walkway there; we stood and walked on air. The glow from the abyss threw light in this place of darkness.

As we stood there Jesus asked me to look closely at the wall of this well. To my surprise, I could see that the wall opened into chambers. There were three tiers of these chambers right underneath the mouth of the well. I could see a thick black curtain hung outside the chambers that segregated them from one another. I found this place to be extremely filthy and foul odor emanated as if there were sewage drains nearby.

Jesus told me that the first two tiers, which consisted of five chambers each, were occupied and used by Satan but the third tier lay unused and was empty. I asked Jesus why this was so. To which He replied, "It is impossible for Satan to use the third tier because of the intense heat from the abyss."

Regarding those ten chambers in the two tiers he explained to me that each chamber represented a particular department in the kingdom of darkness ruled by evil powers devoted to specific tasks. Jesus referred to these evil powers as rulers of darkness.

Jesus said, "Daughter, I will show you the evil, hidden activities of Satan's kingdom which he operates from here."

With that, we entered the first chamber through the partition in the curtain.

For we wrestle not against flesh and blood, but against principalities, against powers, against the rulers of darkness of
this world, against spiritual wickedness in high places.

—EPHESIANS 6:12, KJV

CHAMBER OF APOSTASY AND HERESY

As Jesus and I entered this dark chamber in the well, I could see
a dimly lit lantern that hung by the side. Through its reflection I
could see cobwebs filled the place and how dirty the chamber was.

Satan appeared to be teaching a small class of powerful demons
on what looked like a blackboard. Neither Satan nor the demons
appeared to see us.

Jesus and I moved closer to the blackboard. Jesus asked me to
read what was written on the board. Much to my amazement, I saw
the names of some of the churches around the world written on
the board. Jesus explained to me that these churches I saw on the
board were a threat to Satan. Then He asked me to listen attentively
to what Satan was speaking.

Pointing at these churches, Satan said, "These are the churches
which are a real threat to us. Though there are many churches
throughout the world, we need not worry about those who do
not meddle with us." Then, with a chuckle, he added, "The asleep
churches are not a threat to us. We are only after the uncompromising ones—the ones that expose us by preaching the truth and
snatch away those who belong to us. Hence, we must root out these
churches which are alive." He said those words in immense anger
and in an urgent tone.

As soon as he had finished speaking those words, I saw a screen
appear in front of him. With the touch of a button, the name of
one of the mentioned churches listed on the board appeared on the
screen with complete details, including the country it belonged to,
and the names of the individuals actively involved in the advancement of the gospel in that particular church flashed alongside. Next
on the screen appeared the pastor's name and listed underneath

his name were his weaknesses: fame and money were highlighted in red.

Then, Jesus explained to me, "Satan looks at these weaknesses as 'entry points' for himself. Through these entry points, he will seek to make the pastor compromise with the truth, remove the passion and zeal for My Word, and in the end render him ineffective for My work. The enemy's final aim is always destruction. As you have seen him target the pastor and study his weaknesses, likewise he will also target those individuals whose names you saw appear on the screen. These individuals are members of the church who are dedicated and serious for My service. However, Satan's main focus is on the pastor."

As soon as Jesus finished speaking those words, I heard Satan say to his class, "If we get the pastor, we will get the church." As Jesus had said, the enemy's main focus was the pastor. I marveled to see as Satan and his demons planned to set effective traps based on the pastor's weaknesses to ensnare this particular pastor and destroy this church.

I watched this class of demons clenching their fists, one of whom had the ears and wings of a bat, cry out in immense hatred, "We want his blood!" and "Death to this church!" Looking at his comrades, Satan questioned, "Who will go to destroy this church?" With this question I saw the hands of demons go up as they clamored to volunteer to destroy this church on their hit list.

Jesus told me that these were the demons of apostasy and heresy. These will try to influence the pastor by attacking him in his particular areas of weaknesses so as to make him compromise with what he knows as the truth and attempt to make him fall away from the truth and teach contrary to the Word.

As we watched, I saw Satan select two demons for the assignment and dispatch them to the church. Jesus and I followed them. Suddenly I found us in that church. There was a church service in progress, and I saw the pastor preaching. At that moment I saw those two demons whisper lies in his ears. He did not heed to one but started to listen to the lies of the other. Instantly he began to preach in response to those lies.

Has Satan been whispering lies in your ears to compromise or dilute what you know as the absolute truth in the Bible? Do not give in to those lies. Be aware of any weaknesses that you might have, surrender them at the cross, and ask the Holy Spirit to be your helper, for He alone can help you to live victoriously in this world.

> For if you live according to the flesh you will die; but if by the Spirit you put to death the deeds of the body, you will live.
>
> —ROMANS 8:13

> And take…the sword of the Spirit, which is the word of God; praying always with all prayer and supplication in the Spirit.
>
> —EPHESIANS 6:17–18

Satan does and will exploit your weaknesses if you give him a place in your life. This is not to suggest that he makes you sin. For the Word of God says:

> But each one is tempted when he is drawn away by his own desires and enticed. Then, when desire has conceived, it gives birth to sin; and sin, when it is full-grown, brings forth death.
>
> —JAMES 1:14–15

> And whoso breaketh an hedge, a serpent shall bite him.
>
> —ECCLESIASTES 10:8, KJV

The spiritual battle with the enemy is a very real one. Always be on guard against the attacks of the enemy. Please do not compromise with the truth of God's Word.

I have seen Satan and his demons study in great detail the

weaknesses of a pastor and target those alive churches that are making a difference in the lives of many in bringing them to Christ.

You and your church might be on Satan's hit list. Be watchful against apostasy and heresy so that you do not fall prey to the enemy. His aim is to make you fall away from the truth and teach contrary to the Word.

These demonic spirits cause dissension and disunity among believers within growing churches and cause a great deal of harm to the body of Christ. They do everything within their power and also team up with other demons devoted to other specific tasks— anger, bitterness, jealousy, etc.—in their coordinated attempt to break up active churches. Nothing makes them more happy and satisfied than to see a once alive church lose its liveliness and love for God and His work. Satan seeks to turn these alive churches into asleep churches so that they are no longer a threat to him.

> Lest Satan should take advantage of us; for we are not igno-
> rant of his devices.
> —2 CORINTHIANS 2:11

> Therefore submit to God. Resist the devil and he will flee
> from you.
> —JAMES 4:7

> For the weapons of our warfare are not carnal but mighty
> in God for pulling down strongholds, casting down argu-
> ments and every high thing that exalts itself against the
> knowledge of God, bringing every thought into captivity to
> the obedience of Christ, and being ready to punish all dis-
> obedience when your obedience is fulfilled.
> —2 CORINTHIANS 10:4–6

The next night I was translated instantly in my spirit and found myself with Jesus inside the next chamber that Jesus referred to as the occult chamber.

OCCULT CHAMBER

In this chamber I beheld powerful demons of the occult that waited impatiently and restlessly to be summoned and dispatched to the world.

Jesus explained to me that being masters of deception, these demons can take the form of the deceased and imitate all the characteristics parading as if it were the actual person. However, they are not just limited to the role of imitating the dead; they also can inhabit and possess those involved in any form of occult such as astrology, channeling, divination, fortune telling, magic art, necromancy, tarot reading, spiritism, spiritualism, shamanism, witchcraft, voodoo, etc.

The clairvoyant or the medium does not have special abilities to summon the dead; this happens only because they open themselves to be possessed by these demons of occult and in turn are deceived by them.

As Jesus spoke to me, I saw a red light suddenly flash through this chamber that caused a flutter of excitement among those wicked demons. I marveled to see that these demons waited in queues for their turns to be summoned from earth. With flashing of the red light, two demons started to tussle with each other in spite of the queue; a commotion ensued and the demon that headed the department settled the matter and dispatched the one selected for the assignment.

Jesus told me that at times more than one demon is dispatched to earth according to the summoning from earth. It looked to me something like an order was processed as per the quantity desired. In my curiosity, I asked Jesus, "How do these know how many demons to dispatch to earth since they can not read thoughts, unlike you, Lord?"

Jesus explained to me, "The red beam of light acts as a form of communication from demons on earth. They work in coordination with them to dispatch the required number of demons to earth.

The number of beams reflects the need. What you saw was a single beam, which means one was required. Similarly, two beams would mean two, and so on."

The particular demon selected for the assignment rushed out of the chamber as if exiting the place was a reward in itself. This demon seemed to have a body of a giant-sized thorn.

Jesus held my hand and said, "Daughter, I will show you how these demons deceive people."

With that, I instantly found us in front of a medium. The room was in semidarkness. There were several demons around her, though she seemed to be unaware of their presence. Seated on her right side was a woman. Jesus told me that this woman had lost her husband recently and was heartbroken as a result of his death. In desperation, she had come to this medium to contact her dead husband.

Suddenly I saw a demon (the one I saw dispatched from hell) stand in front of the medium. As I watched, it entered the medium's body and instantly began to speak through her. The client perceived this voice to be that of her late husband. The demon was deceiving her into believing that this was indeed her late husband. The demon referred to her by a particular name, which according to her was known only to her husband. Therefore, she assumed that it was indeed her late husband. The demon continued to deceive her, saying that how much he loved her and missed her and that he was in a much better place and happy. Finally, the demon said that it was time to leave and bid her good-bye, asking her to take care of herself. I could see that the victim was clearly taken in by this deception.

It was at this point that I saw one of the demons that loitered around the medium enter the client. This woman was not only deceived into believing that her husband had actually spoken to her but now she was also inhabited by one of the demons. Meanwhile the medium was deceived into believing that she had channeled the

Chambers in Hell

client's late husband, mistaking the possession as her special ability to contact the dead.

Channelers and others wishing to make a contact with the dead, please listen to me; you are being deceived by these demons. It is impossible for the dead to appear. You are putting yourself in grave danger by practicing this evil.

> There shall not be found among you anyone who makes his son or his daughter pass through the fire, or one who practices witchcraft, or a soothsayer, or one who interprets omens, or a sorcerer, or one who conjures spells, or a medium, or a spiritist, or one who calls up the dead. For all who do these things are an abomination to the LORD.
> —DEUTERONOMY 18:10–12

In doing so you are opening yourselves to be inhabited by these wicked demons. There are no good spirits, and certainly you cannot control them.

Jesus told me that this demon, after this first performance of deception, was on his way for yet another assignment. He said this as He held my hand and asked me to follow Him.

Immediately I found us in a dimly lit room, I could see a woman seated with a candle burning in front of her. Jesus told me that she was trying to make a contact with her dead daughter. I saw this same demon approach the woman and take hold of her hand. Powered by this demon she began immediately to write on a blank sheet of paper. With this automatic writing she was been deceived into believing that she had been successful in making a contact with her dead daughter.

Jesus told me that this demon sent to earth will continue to deceive anyone who will open themselves to this sin. It is his bid to stay here on earth and perform all chores to please his master, Satan. He will also team up with other demons already on earth, if required, to accomplish the given task.

55

Beloved, have nothing to do with occult in any form. Please repent now if you are involved in any form of occult. If you are a person who reads daily horoscopes, that is being involved in occult. Do not dabble with an Ouija board that opens you to the world of demons.

Jesus told that these occult demons can also possess birds and animals for fortune telling. If you have wondered how the birds and animals are able to make accurate predictions, it is certainly not because of special skills that they possess on their own but are powered by these demons.

Jesus said, "Daughter, I will show you more." Instantly, I found us standing in front of a fortune teller who was making use of a parrot to predict the future of the person. As soon as the parrot was let out of its cage, I saw a demon of divination possess this parrot. It then started to pick a series of cards, one at a time, in its beak. I could see another demon that stood near the fortune-teller who gave him the interpretation behind those cards that signified specific events in the client's life. The fortune-teller simply passed on this information received by the demon to the client. The client agreed and accepted the information given regarding his past and present as "accurate." Thus, having secured his trust, in like manner the parrot went on to predict the man's future by picking a series of those cards powered by the demon of divination.

Beloved, it is not difficult for these demons to gather all information about your past and present and thereby secure your trust. It is God alone who knows your future. Put your trust in God. Repent sincerely if you have ever participated in any form of occult.

Soon after I found us in front of a New Age channeler who appeared to be speaking to her spirit guide. She kept referring to her spirit guide as Master Jesus Christ. She was blinded by this demon that presented himself as Master Jesus Christ and was deceived into believing that this demon was actually Jesus Christ. This being of light that appeared to this woman was not the Jesus Christ of the Bible; I saw that firsthand. Do not marvel, for these demons can take any form to deceive you, even the form of Jesus Christ. "And no wonder! For Satan himself transforms himself into an angel of light" (2 Cor. 11:14). Do not be lured by this trap of the devil.

The Bible is clear that no man can serve two masters (Matt. 6:24). New Age practitioners, please listen; Jesus Christ is not *a* way but the *only* way. He is the one true God. Do not be deceived by the enemy. This New Age Jesus that might appear to you is not Jesus Christ of the Bible but a demon. There is no fellowship of light with darkness: "For what fellowship has righteousness with lawlessness? And what communion has light with darkness?" (2 Cor. 6:14). Please repent now. Jesus Christ, who is the way, the truth, and the life, told me to warn you before it is too late.

Right after this Jesus took me to another part of the globe. I found we were in an auditorium where psychic healings were taking place. I saw several demons encircling a psychic healer; among them were two that appeared as wise old men. I asked Jesus about them. Jesus referred to these wise old men as the spiritual hosts of the enemy in high places. He also said that the devil deceives many people into believing that the wise old man is Him (Jesus Christ). Beloved, if there is a wise old man appearing to you and you believe that it is Jesus Christ, be warned. This figure that appears to you and strengthens your belief that Jesus is *one* of the ways to God is not Jesus Christ of the Bible but a demon. No matter if this demon even takes the form of Jesus Himself, do not be deceived.

As I continued to watch, these spiritual hosts of the enemy that appeared as wise old men, one on either side of the psychic healer, gave instructions to other demons to assist this psychic healer in healing. It seemed to me that this event took place under their watchful eyes and they were the ones in actual control of the event; the psychic healer was merely carrying out their plans.

This psychic healer was deceived into believing that energy flowed through her hands and she had special abilities to heal people. I saw two demons come over her hands; and powered by these evil forces, she began to lay hands on people and claimed that they were getting healed. In that crowd of people who had gathered there for the healing, I could see a woman who had a problem in her liver. This healer summoned her and laid her hands on this woman. As soon as she laid her hands on that woman, I saw the woman's problem in the liver shift down to her ankle.

Beloved, Satan and his demons do not have the power to heal; they merely shift the point of ailment to another part of the body. I have seen this myself. This woman was deceived since her ailment shifted from the liver and gave her the impression that she was healed indeed. But then she began to complain of the pain in the ankle. The psychic healer meanwhile maintained that the woman was healed.

Jesus told me that these demons of occult also team up with other demons already in the world devoted to specific tasks such as anger, bitterness, jealousy, self-pity, depression, etc., for the completion of given tasks as required.

Jesus said to me, "Daughter, I will show you how this works." And instantly I found us in yet another part of the world in front of a man who was calling on higher powers to assist him in a particular task. He seemed to be oblivious to our presence.

Jesus told me that this man was a voodoo practitioner and was placing a death curse on a man. He was conjuring powerful demons to assist him in this work. After a while I saw two powerful demons arrive at the scene. Jesus took my hand and said, "Come with Me." Instantly I found we were in a house. I could see a young man in that house who appeared to be lost in a deep thought. Jesus told me that this young man was the one cursed to death by the voodoo practitioner. Suddenly I saw those two demons enter this house and start to whisper in the man's ears. One of them said, "Your life is worthless," while another said, "There is no point in living." And then they said together, "Kill yourself." The victim, without a question, accepted those voices as his own thoughts and proceeded to end his life. The occult demon teamed up with the demon of depression and influenced the victim to kill himself and thereby achieved their purpose. These demons deemed this victim as a "prized" soul for their master Satan that assured a reward from him.

These strategies of the enemy have been effective over the years. Unless you are born again and live in obedience to God's Word, the weapons of warfare provided by God as mentioned in the Bible will not be effective against the enemy.

> Stand therefore, having girded your waist with truth, having put on the breastplate of righteousness, and having shod your feet with the preparation of the gospel of peace; above all, taking the shield of faith with which you will be able to quench all the fiery darts of the wicked one. And take the helmet of salvation, and the sword of the Spirit, which is the word of God.
>
> —Ephesians 6:14–17

Make sure that you live this life pleasing in God's sight in holiness that ensures being effectively equipped with His armor to defeat the enemy.

Many times murders, suicides, etc., take place in like manner. These demons also throng in great numbers to those places where murders, suicides, etc., take place and mark them as their territories. These territories can be identified as having an affinity to certain activity of sin like suicides, immorality, murders, etc. This also explains notorious crimes that take place in certain areas. I have seen demons go berserk over the sight of human blood. Again, they do not make people sin but influence and encourage evil desires and passions, particularly if the person has opened himself or herself for them.

Voodoo practitioners, please take note; you are controlled by these demons who are achieving their purposes through you. Please repent; for if you die in this state, you will end up in hell and these demons who work for you now will torment you in hell.

Occult practitioners, the ones you are working for—Satan and his demons—do not want to be punished in hell, which was pre-pared for them. Why should you end up there where Satan and his demons do not want to go? Please repent and renounce your sins, and Jesus will receive you. While alive, you have an opportunity to come to Jesus; after death it is too late.

Also, Satan tries to destroy those Christians in the body of Christ who are a threat to him. If he has failed in his repeated attempts to destroy a Christian, He sends those more wicked and powerful occult demons from his kingdom to achieve his purpose. These demons work in addition to those already operating in earth against that Christian. Satan's purpose is destruction. If you are a genuine Christian and wondering why all hell has broken loose against you, this may be the reason. Does everything seem to have gone wrong suddenly? Is there no sign of progress and fruitfulness in anything that you do? Working with other demons, these demons will con-jure people and situations against you to destroy you emotionally, financially, mentally, and spiritually.

Remember, no matter how powerless you appear to be in front of this situation, you have the power in the name of Jesus to bind these demons. Keep praying; march ahead and you will eventually see the victory. No matter how powerful these demons appear to be, they bow down and are powerless in front of Jesus Christ our Savior and King of kings.

SECRET PACT CHAMBER

The next night I was instantly translated in my spirit and taken to the third chamber. Jesus told me that in this chamber secret pacts took place with Satan to attain fame, money, and power in the world.

This chamber was also dimly lit and filthy. I beheld a pastor make a secret pact with Satan to attain fame, money, and power. I was horrified to see that such a thing could even exist. Jesus told me sadly that there are many like this pastor in the world who have sold Him in exchange for fame, money, and power.

These pastors are ravenous wolves though they come in sheep's clothing (Matt. 7:15). Their pious appearance on the outside is a deception and far from reality. These compromise the Word of God by diluting the power of the gospel resulting in its corruption and making it of no effect. Thereby they mislead many from the truth.

As I looked at this pastor, I was reminded when Jesus Himself was tempted by Satan.

> The devil took Him up on an exceedingly high mountain, and showed Him all the kingdoms of the world and their glory. And he said to Him, "All these things I will give You if You will fall down and worship me." Then Jesus said to him, "Away with you, Satan! For it is written, 'You shall worship the Lord your God, and Him only you shall serve.'"
>
> —MATTHEW 4:8–10

If you happen to be like the pastor mentioned above, please repent.

Judas Iscariot, the disciple of Jesus Christ, sold his Master. When he realized what he had done, he went back to the Pharisees to return those pieces of silver. They refused to accept it back and he ended up killing himself.

> Then Judas, His betrayer, seeing that He had been condemned, was remorseful and brought back the thirty pieces of silver to the chief priests and elders, saying, "I have sinned by betraying innocent blood." And they said, "What is that to us? You see to it!" Then he threw down the pieces of silver in the temple and departed, and went and hanged himself.
>
> —MATTHEW 27:3–5

He need not have done so. If he came back to Jesus Christ, he would have been forgiven.

Beloved, have you sold your master, Jesus Christ for money, fame, or power? Whatever the reason you have sold Him, remember it will add to your torment just like Judas. He loathed that money so much that he wanted to get rid of it somehow, to the point of going back to the very same people to whom he had sold Jesus in an attempt to return those pieces of silver—the reason for which he had betrayed his master. He hung himself, burdened with the guilt the betrayal brought him.

Beloved, the silver pieces were the price of blood or blood money (Matt. 27:6). Whatever you have traded Jesus for, whether money, fame, or power, you will be guilty of *His* blood—that innocent life who gave Himself for you. However, you do not have to resort to what Judas Iscariot did. Please repent, come back to Jesus, and He will forgive you.

> If we confess our sins, He is faithful and just to forgive us our sins and to cleanse us from all unrighteousness.
> —1 JOHN 1:9

Jesus and I moved away in sadness from this chamber.

CHAMBER OF TORMENT

I found us in front of yet another chamber. I could hear loud screams of men and women emanate from this chamber. Jesus told me that it is here that His children are tormented by Satan. Satan calls this his torment chamber.

As I pondered over this statement of Jesus, He spoke again: "Do you not remember, daughter, that you have been here already in April 2000?" As soon as Jesus said that, the horrific scene of the painful ordeal that I went through in April 2000 flashed before my eyes. All these years I had asked Jesus regarding the place where I had endured these things, but all that He would say was that I went to a part of hell. Today He was answering my query, and I understood that I was tormented by those demons in this chamber.

Those Christians who are serious in their walk with Christ at times are expressly allowed by God to be tested. As mentioned in the Book of Job, Satan was granted permission by God to strip Job of his possessions and his family and to afflict him with excruciating boils.

> Satan went out from the presence of the LORD, and struck Job with painful boils from the sole of his foot to the crown of his head. And he took for himself a potsherd with which to scrape himself while he sat in the midst of the ashes.
>
> —JOB 2:7–8

Though Satan is bent on destruction, particularly of those who have given themselves completely for God's cause, it is important to understand that he is also limited by God's permission as found in the Book of Job.

> So Satan answered the LORD and said, "Does Job fear God for nothing? Have You not made a hedge around him, around his household, and around all that he has on every side? You have blessed the work of his hands, and his possessions have increased in the land. But now, stretch out Your hand and touch all that he has, and he will surely curse You to Your face!" And the LORD said to Satan, "Behold, all that he has is in your power; only do not lay a hand on his person." So Satan went out from the presence of the LORD.
>
> —JOB 1:9–12

Since character is important in God's eyes, He decided to test Job in order to see his commitment to Him under adversity. The more uncompromising you are in regard to your commitment to God, the more severe your torment will be.

One early morning at 1:00 a.m., as per the time on the bedside clock, I found myself instantly translated in my spirit to this chamber. This chamber was dimly lit, and I saw myself stand in a queue. I noticed that there was another queue next to mine that was longer than mine. This was a wait to be tormented at the hands of demons. Standing in both the queues were men and women of all nationalities and race. I could see them tormented at the hands of powerful demons and their dreadful screams filled that place. As I waited for my turn to be tormented at the hands of these demons, a deep fear gripped my heart; there was no way I could escape from there, it was impossible. Suddenly I saw two huge demons approach me. I could see that these demons had tremendously long nails. Paralyzed with fear, my feet felt heavy like lead, unable to move let alone run. They came near me and touched my skin with their long nails. The moment their nails touched my skin, a sharp burning sensation seeped through my body, I felt as if my entire being was on fire, and soon I was crying out in immense pain.

Seeing me cry, these demons laughed. I could see that they were specially assigned to torture me and thoroughly enjoyed doing so. The more I pleaded with them to stop the torment, the more they laughed. I felt utterly helpless and lost in that place, wondering how I ended up there in the first place and how long the torment would last. To make matters worse, I was looking for Jesus but He was not there. Amidst my loud sobs because of the excruciating pain I underwent, I seriously began to worry whether I would ever be able to get out of that horrible place of continual torture with no respite whatsoever.

At that moment of misery, I noticed an older gentleman of a different nationality next to me; he was tormented by demons as well. Unlike me, he appeared to be unmoved by his circumstances; he was calm and in silent prayer. He looked at me and said, "Pray in tongues and they will not be able to harm you." Encouraged by this statement, I mustered all my strength, ignoring my pain, and began to praise God in my heavenly language.

This enraged the two demons, the ones assigned to torment me, and they began to threaten me with dire consequences if I did not stop immediately. Meanwhile the stranger advised me not to listen to them for they are liars. So I continued to pray and praise God, and these two demons seemed to be unable to harm me anymore and left.

At that point I looked across the chamber and my eyes were drawn to a round black table that looked like a conference table. I could see that Satan was seated as the leader with four other powerful and wicked demons. I also saw that it was Satan who gave instructions to mete out those awful torments and the demons were merely carrying out his orders. As soon as those demons left me, Satan commanded the rest of his pack to torture me. One by one they came, each more wicked and powerful than the other, but I continued to pray and saw that they were unable to harm me further. So they left as they came, one by one.

Those demons appeared darker than the darkness and were twelve feet tall. Suddenly I heard God's voice that instructed me to go home, much to my relief. He guided me to exit that place through a small window within the chamber. The very next moment I found myself in the bed. I looked at the bedside clock to see what time it was. I was shocked to learn that it was already five in the morning. This terrible ordeal had lasted for four hours, and it appeared like a matter of minutes. This spiritual experience resulted in a physical manifestation of exhaustion I could not explain; I had never experienced one like this before. I had no ounce of strength left in the body, coupled with exhaustion, and accompanied by terrible writhing pain all over the body. As a result, my entire day was spent in bed.

My battle with the enemy was a real one; and it is significant to mention that after this experience problems in my life increased by leaps and bounds. Also, Satan visited me in person and said that he would take everything from me if I would still continue to serve Jesus. After this visit of Satan, all hell broke loose in my life. In the following years, as I underwent inexplicable calamities in life, Satan visited me three more times. My circumstances seemed to dampen further yet in the midst of these discouraging and traumatic experiences in which I lost all, I learned to trust God patiently while awaiting the resolution of my problems. Today, I can testify gladly that I emerged victorious out of the entire painful ordeal. "You have turned my mourning into joyful dancing" (Ps. 30:11, NLT).

Beloved, at that time I could not understand this suffering that I had to go through. The reasons were known only to God and it appeared so abnormal in size and duration. I was totally committed to God's will for my life, and I never questioned His will for me; yet my mind failed to understand why those things should happen in my life. You may not be able to see this invisible battle with your eyes, but you will pay a price as a result of that battle in real life.

Are you undergoing a similar unexplained suffering in your life today that you do not understand? No matter how severe your torment appears, never assume that God does not care about you or has deserted you. God sees far more than you can see, and He is teaching you valuable lessons beyond your present understanding that you will come to cherish in times ahead.

> And we know that all things work together for good to those who love God, to those who are the called according to His purpose.
>
> —Romans 8:28

If you do not shrink back at this time of suffering, bear it patiently, and persevere at the end of it all, you will come out much stronger in God as your character is built in Him. And also you will see God bless you doubly as Job: "Indeed the Lord gave Job twice as much as he had before" (Job 42:10).

Chamber of Slumber

We moved over to this next chamber and entered inside. Once inside the chamber, I could see an enormous hairy demon that appeared to be asleep. Jesus told me that this was the chamber of slumber and the hairy demon ruled this department. I saw other demons there that appeared to be asleep, too. Jesus told me that their character symbolized their appearance.

Jesus said to me that the demon ruling this department was waiting to receive instructions from Satan to carry out his assignment. On the orders of Satan, he will dispatch those demons to earth to induce sleep to those active Christians who are becoming a threat for him. He will also hinder the spiritual progress in new believers by sending distractions along their ways that help to induce slumber in their lives.

Satan uses these demons to induce slumber to active Christians so as to make them inactive for the expansion of God's kingdom. The aim of inducing sleep in Christians is to cause them to lose their interest, make them unfruitful, and lead them to their spiritual death. Satan achieves this through a number of ways, such as the Bible mentions "he who hears the word, and the cares of this world and deceitfulness of riches choke the word, and he becomes unfruitful" (Matt. 13:22).

Reader, were you an active Christian before and suddenly have grown cold for God? Have the cares of this world or deceitfulness of riches choked the Word in your life? Or there might be some other reason. Whatever the reason for your coldness, it is time to come back to God. The Bible says, "Resist the devil and he will flee from you" (James 4:7).

Do not allow the enemy to have victory over your life. Resist him in the name of Jesus Christ and he will flee from you. If you give the enemy a foothold in your life, he will not just make you unfruitful but he will also destroy you in the end. Please repent and come back to Jesus Christ. It is time to shrug off your sleep.

CHAMBER OF DEPRESSION

I was translated in my spirit and found myself inside this chamber next to Jesus. I could see a giant-sized demon inside who appeared to wail and beat his chest as if in distress. I wondered what could be the reason behind his apparent distress.

Just then Jesus began to explain to me, "Daughter, this is the chamber of depression and this demon that you see wail and lament heads this particular department. He has several demons working under him and is waiting to receive orders from Satan to carry out his assignment. His appearance is figurative of the function he performs. This demon purposes to attack those Christians who are making a meaningful difference in the lives of many, such as influential pastoral leaders. This demon works with other demons to achieve his purpose. If given a place in life, he will destroy the person. This demon has destroyed many meaningful lives."

As Jesus spoke those words, He held my hand and said, "Come with Me. I will show you one of its many victims." Instantly I found us in a different part of hell standing in front of a cell.

I could see a lost soul of a man inside the cell. Jesus told me that he was a pastor when alive and was also used of Him. As I looked at this once popular face, he saw Jesus and in immense pain turned to look at Him.

This lost soul began to speak, "I was so depressed. I really did love my wife and children but I made big mistakes; big mistakes!"

Then Jesus answered, "Depression ruled you and you went back to the addiction from which I once set you free; that killed you in the end. If only you had repented, you will not be here today. I waited for you to come back to Me. I gave you many chances right till your end came, but you did not heed Me and ended up here."

Upon hearing what Jesus said, this lost soul wept bitterly and said, "I even preached about this place."

As we moved away sadly from this cell, I saw another cell right next to it similar in appearance but unoccupied. Jesus stopped in front of this empty cell and looked at it. He said suddenly, "Daughter, if you had given into depression, you would have been here." That statement of Jesus hit me hard as those scenes of my life when I went through hard times flashed before my eyes. Committed to God's will in spite of adverse circumstances as calamities stuck me one by one, the devil had whispered in my ears many times, "All that you live for, is only for God. You do not deserve a pitiful life such as this. Look what God has done; He has let you down. It is better for you to be dead than alive." Thank God I did not heed to the voice of the devil. If I had, I would have been right there in that cell.

You might be a pastor and serving God sincerely. Has a tragedy befallen you in your life? Has the devil been whispering in your ears to throw in your towel? Is he telling you to forsake God and die? He may tell you this himself or use circumstances or people whom you count very close to you, such as your spouse. As Job's wife, who said to him, "Do you still hold fast to your integrity? Curse God and die!" (Job 2:9). Job lost everything he had, including his children; and at that moment of utter depression, Satan used his wife to question his integrity, curse God, and die.

You must know that Satan is adept in stepping up his virulent attacks against you if you happen to be genuinely committed to God's service. He can use anybody, as mentioned in Job's example, even your spouse to destroy you emotionally, physically, financially, and spiritually. Also, if you happen to give in to this demon of depression, it will team up with other wicked demons and bring back old sinful addictions that you gave up after coming to Christ and they will kill you in the end. You might be facing a raging storm in your life right now, but do not give in to the lies of the enemy to quit, to end it all; for if you do, you will end up in those unoccupied cells of torment in hell. "Therefore submit to God. Resist the devil and he will flee from you" (James 4:7).

CHAMBER OF PERVERSION

The next night Jesus appeared to me and said, "Daughter, I need to show you more." With that I was instantly translated in my spirit and found myself standing with Jesus in front of another chamber. I could smell the revolting foul stench unlike anything I had come across before in hell that seemed to emanate from this chamber.

As we entered this chamber, Jesus told me, "Daughter, this is the chamber of perversion." I felt this overpowering nauseating stench, and I wanted out of that place as soon as possible. Unable to contain it any longer, finally I asked Jesus, "Lord, why does it smell so awful in here?"

Jesus replied, "Daughter, as My life produces a sweet-smelling aroma in all those well pleasing in My sight, similarly, sin bears an aroma of death. It stinks." I understood then that the revolting stench portrayed the abomination in the sight of God.

I could see that the chamber was dimly lit. I saw a huge-sized demon inside this chamber that kept changing its form from a male to a female, and at times he appeared both male and female at the same time. Jesus told me that this demon of perversion ruled this specific area and had several demons working under him. This demon in charge of this department was waiting to receive instructions from earth to dispatch those working under him to earth and seduce those Christian men, women, and their families who were practicing holy lives, to make them fall in sin.

I noticed that in this chamber working under the huge demon were many demons present in a significantly larger number than the other chambers. These demons, also appearing as seductive men or women and at times as both a man and a woman, were waiting to be sent to earth on being summoned. I saw them engage in such acts of perversion with other demons that are too gross to mention.

As soon as Jesus said those words, I saw beams of red light flash through this grotesque chamber. They were five in number, the highest I had seen in any other chamber. As five of these demons rushed out squealing in delight, I heard the demon that headed the department utter with laughter, "Destroy them!" Their aim was to destroy Christian homes and marriages, to ruin Christian testimonies, and to cause disgrace.

Jesus told me with sadness, "These are being dispatched to My children to destroy them." He then began to weep in grief and said, "Many of my once saved children are slaves of this sin."

He held my hand and asked me to follow Him. I instantly found us in a home. As I looked around, I knew it was a Christian home as I could see a lot of scripture verses within this home. Then Jesus told me that this was a pastor's home. At that moment I saw a lovely couple emerge out of their bedroom. Jesus told me that was the pastor and his wife. After a while I saw the wife of the pastor leave the house.

As soon as she left, I heard her husband say excitedly, "Now is my moment," and hurriedly proceeded to switch on the computer, He said, "I cannot be without this." To my disbelief and shock, he was watching pornography. Jesus turned His face away, and I could see tears trickle from His eyes. He led me out of that place quickly and said, "This pastor is a slave of pornography." Sadly, the pastor had not realized Jesus Christ was his unseen guest that day, the One he had turned away.

Beloved, make sure you do not turn away Jesus, the unseen guest, with your sin.

Jesus said to me, "I have to show you more." I instantly found us standing in front of a cathedral. I could see that there was a lone car parked in the parking area. Jesus said to me, "A grave sin is taking place here." We began to walk toward the car. As we almost reached where the car stood, I could see a man and woman inside that car involved in an illicit relationship. Jesus put His hands to His face, covered His eyes, and sobbed. Then He said, "This man is a pastor, a married man, and a father to two sons. That woman is a member of the church. As a cover-up for their adulterous relationship, they meet each other under the pretext of Bible study and counseling." We moved away quickly from that spot. I was horrified to hear what Jesus had said. As we walked away He said, "They have made My house 'a den of thieves' (Matt. 21:13). Daughter, tell My children that I desire truth in the inward parts" (Ps. 51:6).

Pastors, if this is your story, repent. Be true to God in your calling, be faithful to your spouse, and set an example for others to follow.

> While they promise them liberty, they themselves are slaves of corruption; for by whom a person is overcome, by him also he is brought into bondage. For if, after they have escaped the pollutions of the world through the knowledge of the Lord and Savior Jesus Christ, they are again entangled in them and overcome, the latter end is worse for them than the beginning. For it would have been better for them not to have known the way of righteousness, than having known it, to turn from the holy commandment delivered to them.
>
> —2 PETER 2:19–21

Beloved, do not give a place to the devil in your life; he will rob you of everything—your home, your family, also your testimony—resulting in your ruin.

Your body is for God's glory because it is the temple of God.

> Flee sexual immorality. Every sin that a man does is outside the body, but he who commits sexual immorality sins against his own body. Or do you not know that your body is the temple of the Holy Spirit who is in you, whom you have from God, and you are not your own?
>
> —1 CORINTHIANS 6:18–19

I was grieved in my spirit after witnessing the two incidents; and added to that agony, was to see Jesus cry. It was so heartbreaking.

Just then, Jesus began to speak, "Daughter, there are a few of My remnant who do not give into the seducing of these demons."

As soon as He spoke these words, I found us in front of a young woman knelt down in prayer. As I watched I saw two demons of perversion come to tempt her; but standing on the Word of God, she resisted them and they fled from her presence. But still they kept an eye on her. Each time they came near, I saw her resist them and saw them flee as a result.

Jesus said, "The battle with the enemy is ongoing and he will by all means try to corrupt those who live for Me and are pure in My sight. These seducing spirits of perversion also attack My children when they are asleep. When all their attempts to tempt one to sin have been met with resistance, these unclean spirits attempt to sow the sin of sexual immorality within My children when asleep. This is done in order to arouse sinful desires within the individual and lead him or her to sin when all the attempts to do so have failed otherwise. These attacks of the enemy must be resisted to live victoriously." "Therefore, take heed lest you fall" (1 Cor. 10:12).

Men and women of God, are you victims of this demon of perversion? Do not give it a place in your life, for it seeks to make you sin by arousing evil passions within you to make you unholy and take you away from the presence of God. If you have such an experience while asleep in the night, you will wake up to find those sinful passions wanting to take control of you which prior to the experience were absent inside of you. These unclean spirits through such attacks seek to open you to those particular sins of immorality, which earlier may have never even come across your mind. After this experience, new to you, you will find yourself inclined to such evil sins. Do not give it a place in your life. Remember, you do not have to be a victim and taken advantage of when asleep; resist this demon in Jesus' name and he will flee from you.

> For the weapons of our warfare are not carnal but mighty
> in God for pulling down strongholds, casting down

arguments and every high thing that exalts itself against the knowledge of God, bringing every thought into captivity to the obedience of Christ.

—2 Corinthians 10:4–5

Reader, do you happen to struggle with immoral thoughts, pornography, etc.? Please repent and be set free from these addictions. Remember God watches what you do in secret. "Pursue righteousness, godliness, faith," as mentioned in 1 Timothy 6:11, "for to be carnally minded is death, but to be spiritually minded is life and peace" (Rom. 8:6).

If you give a place in your life to these immoral spirits, they will enslave you and lead you to your disastrous end.

Remember that Satan is constantly working to ruin your marriage, family, and also your testimony. Beloved, you can overcome the adversary by living in holiness for the blood of the innocent lamb and word of your testimony to be effective against the enemy. "And they overcame him by the blood of the Lamb and by the word of their testimony" (Rev. 12:11).

If you are married, cherish your marriage and marriage partner given of the Lord. Be true and love your partner as Christ loves the church, for marriage is an image of God's unity with His body, the church.

Pursue peace with all people, and holiness, without which no one will see the Lord.

—Hebrews 12:14

Be an example to the believers in word, in conduct, in love, in spirit, in faith, in purity.

—1 Timothy 4:12

If you happen to be a slave to this sin, repent sincerely and renounce it, asking Jesus to set you free from this sin so that you will be free indeed. Be the one that emits a sweet fragrance for God through your life and not a stench.

CHAMBER OF FEAR

The next night again I was instantly translated and found myself beside Jesus in a yet another chamber. Jesus said to me that this was the chamber of fear.

Suddenly there was a deafening loud explosion like that of an eruption of lava. With Jesus beside me, I was not afraid. Moreover, He held my hand as a refreshing assurance of His presence.

This chamber was dimly lit like all others and appeared smaller than the other chambers. I could see a powerful demon in this chamber, and he seemed to be holding a snare in between the sharp claws of his hands. He seemed to be thoroughly engrossed in what appeared sort of role-playing with other demons that were short in stature. They did not appear to see us.

These small-sized demons had humanlike faces but animal-like bodies. They were running about in circles, giving the demon with a snare quite a chase as he attempted to ensnare them.

He did succeed in ensnaring some. As he held them captive one by one and tightened the loop around each, he snarled, "Mission accomplished." I did not see him ever give up on those who managed to escape his clutches, but he constantly attempted to capture them somehow.

As I watched intrigued, I could see that he finally managed to capture one of them on the run and proudly displayed his prized catch, similar to a hunter who displays his prized game with pride.

Their role-playing appeared so natural that it could have been mistaken for a real event. As I watched engrossed, suddenly Jesus began to explain to me what this was all about. He said, "Daughter, the demon with the snare rules this department of fear. The others playing the role of preyed-upon humans are the ones that work under him. These demons will torment the humans they are assigned to once dispatched from here.

Their game is figurative of the function they perform in the kingdom of darkness. There are many Christians who fall easy prey to fear. There are a few strong ones who avoid being ensnared and manage to escape from the enemy but he does not give up on them so easily. As you see, he keeps trying till he succeeds, after which he displays the captive as the "prized" catch for his master in an effort to please him and in anticipation of a reward.

While Satan aims to prey upon on all born-again Christians and gets most of the prey easily, his eyes are on the stronger ones, those who are tough, who do not give in easily to the lure of his trap. But he keeps trying and waits for their strength to run out at some point in order to catch them at their weakest—when the strong are not so strong anymore.

Those who let themselves to be enticed and trapped by the enemy's snare are brought under the bondage of fear. Once under this bondage, they are lost in the sea of hopelessness and stripped of their trust in Me, resulting in a complete distrust of My grace, goodness, power, and providence. Ruled by fear, these quit the divine vision that they were once committed to; and thereafter take a turn for the worse. All that is needed to overcome this battle is to make use of the weapon of faith provided to them and rejoice in victory which comes eventually if they would only persevere."

As soon as Jesus finished speaking those words, I found us instantly in another land. We watched a man ready to leave with all his belongings loaded in a nearby van. He did not appear to see us.

Jesus said sadly, "Daughter, I called him to this place to serve Me, but he is ready to quit this place for good. As things did not work out as per his expectations, he decided the place was not good enough for him. Instead of letting fear rule him, if only he had trusted Me with his needs, he need not have made this decision and also would have fulfilled what I called him to do."

Beloved, have you been ensnared by this demon of fear? Have

you quit the vision God laid in your heart and as a result that divine mission remains incomplete?

> That they may come to their senses and escape the snare of
> the devil, having been taken captive by him to do his will.
> —2 TIMOTHY 2:26

I urge you earnestly to get back to that vision God laid in your heart empowered by faith. Remember, this battle is for real and there is no time to sit back and let yourself be ensnared by the enemy. The enemy is constantly working to accomplish his missions and you cannot quit the divine vision. If you do so, you hand him over the victory in your life. Also, the work of God in your life will remain unaccomplished because you decided to quit the divine vision.

No matter what arrows the enemy is throwing your way, do not quit your vision. "Where there is no vision, the people perish" (Prov. 29:18, KJV).

If only you would persevere for a little while and stay on ground, you will see the victory. So do not walk away from that victory that God has for you if you only tarry.

If you give in to fear, it will torment you and make your life miserable, quench your joy, and eventually lead you to change the course of your direction away from God's purpose for your life. You might be in a challenging and difficult circumstance today but take heart:

> God is faithful; he will not let you be tempted beyond what
> you can bear. But when you are tempted, he will also pro-
> vide a way out so that you can endure it.
> —1 CORINTHIANS 10:13, NIV

Beloved, you may be placed in an unpleasant situation, much against your expectation, yet tarry and submit to God; one day your vision will bear fruit.

God uses difficult situations in our lives to mold us further in His image. His pruning may not be pleasant, but it results in bearing much fruit for Him. "Every branch that bears fruit He prunes, that it may bear more fruit" (John 15:2).

Instead of giving in to fear at this difficult period of time, trust God for all your provisions and fight the good fight of faith.

> Fight the good fight of faith, lay hold on eternal life, to which you were also called and have confessed the good confession in the presence of many witness.
>
> —1 Timothy 6:12

Submit to God at this time and trust Him. The one who has called you is faithful. If you persevere for a while, you will experience the hand of God's deliverance and the blessing as a result of this.

> And what more shall I say? For the time would fail me to tell of Gideon and Barak and Samson and Jephthah, also of David and Samuel and the prophets: who through faith subdued kingdoms, worked righteousness, obtained promises, stopped the mouths of lions, quenched the violence of fire, escaped the edge of the sword, out of weakness were made strong, became valiant in battle, turned to flight the armies of the aliens.
>
> —Hebrews 11:32–34

Satan's Conference Chamber

The next night I was instantly translated in my spirit and found myself next to Jesus in front of this chamber. Jesus said that it is here that Satan holds important discussions with his demons related to his kingdom.

Without stepping inside this chamber, Jesus went past it. As I wondered about this, He looked at me; He knew my thoughts and answered, "Daughter, I will bring you here at an appropriate time when it is in operation. It is empty now."

I also noticed a small group of demons who seemed to be waiting outside certain chambers to be summoned. Curious, I asked Jesus why this was so. He explained to me, "These demons you see waiting outside specific departments do not belong to any particular department but attach themselves with a department for a specific purpose to perform certain roles as required. This is the reason you see demons of guilt wait outside the department of depression. Similarly, other demons with specific roles such as anger, pride, etc., can be called upon by any department as required; hence, the reason for their wait."

In this small group of demons, I also saw giant-sized scorpions. I asked Jesus in bewilderment, "Dear Lord, what are these huge scorpions doing here?"

Jesus said to me, "Daughter, these are demons in the form of scorpions who oppress My children. These attack those children of Mine who are actively engaged in spiritual warfare against them and therefore are a threat to the enemy. By inflicting deadly pain and terror, these demons weigh down the victim and exercise power over them in an all-out effort to curb his or her successful advancement against the kingdom of darkness. These demons work with other demons and incite individuals and situations against the victim. My children have been given authority to trample the adversary in My name."

> Behold, I give you the authority to trample on serpents and scorpions and over all the power of the enemy. And nothing shall by any means hurt you.
> —Luke 10:19

Beloved, are you a Christian warrior going through exceptionally difficult and unexplained situations? You might be under the oppression of the enemy. Remember, you have the power over the adversary in the name of Jesus. Make use of that authority to see the ultimate victory in your life.

Among this group of demons, I was surprised to see a demon of laziness. Jesus explained that this demon works alongside the spirit of slumber and makes His children lethargic for His work. In the process, they lose their enthusiasm for Him. Saying this, Jesus stopped in front of what appeared to be the tenth chamber. Jesus confirmed this by saying, "This is the last chamber."

RECORD CHAMBER

As we walked inside this chamber, Jesus said to me that this chamber contained the records of all those who belong to Satan around the world. Like all the other chambers, this was dimly lit too. I could see that the length of this chamber exceeded many times its breadth. I saw a dusty small black table with two legs in the chamber but unaccompanied by any chair. Also, I could see two piles of files on this table. This chamber resembled a dirty, unkempt office with streams of black files that gathered dust. Most were scattered around while some were stacked in rows. There was nobody present in this chamber.

Jesus told me that though Satan maintains his own record book, these files that I saw were maintained by his demons. Saying thus, Jesus picked up three files that had gathered dust in that cobweb-laden chamber and asked me to have a look at them. I could see that these files were badly maintained with overwritings and incomplete information. I wondered why this was.

At that moment I saw a demon enter the chamber with a black file. He seemed to grumble like an irked worker. I also noticed that this file that he was carrying was new. He did not appear to see us. I saw him place this file among those scattered files lying around within the chamber.

I could see that there was no alphabetical order to maintain these files, if that could be termed maintained in the first place; it was more out of formality as it appeared. These files were just placed somewhere, whether scattered or stacked in the chamber.

I asked Jesus about this new file and He explained to me saying, "Each time a child is born to those who belong to Satan, he enters that information in his record." I understood then that the new file belonged to a newborn.

Now my attention shifted to the small pile of files stacked on the table. I wondered whether these files held any significance, judging by the way they were kept. Jesus knew my thoughts and explained, "Daughter, these files belong to those who were once sinners but now are born again—My children who are alive on earth."

I saw that in this small pile there were two files that appeared tattered, indicating that they were very old. I could not understand why these files were not discarded in the first place since these belonged to those who were not Satan's children anymore. Jesus again answered my unspoken question: "Satan does not give up so easily and keeps trying his best to get these souls back in his fold. He also keeps looking at these files time to time, hoping that these will come back to him eventually."

I also saw the huge pile of new black files placed next to this small pile on the table. I wondered about these new files. Jesus began to explain to me with sadness, "These files belong to those alive on earth who were once My children but have gone back to Satan." It was disheartening to see that these files were many times more in number in comparison to those who had left Satan's fold.

At that moment I saw two demons enter the place and frantically search for a particular file. One of them kept mentioning the name of a particular person, followed by the name of the country the person belonged to. And the demon said that this person was already there and master (referring to Satan) was asking for the person's file. Jesus explained to me that the mentioned person of the particular country was dead and had been brought to hell already. These demons were looking for this person's file. Jesus said to me that though Satan maintains his record book, at times he called for these files maintained by the demons.

As their search for the particular file continued, I heard one of them suggest to the other to make way to Satan with someone else's file. To that the second demon replied, "No, last time master [Satan] reprimanded me for that mistake." I could sense the fear apparent within him of being disciplined by Satan.

Though it would be humanly impossible to go through the whole lot of files in the chamber within a short span of time, it appeared they did so in a matter of minutes. I beheld these two demons go through the entire collection of files in the record chamber in search for the mentioned person's file within a short time.

As their search process continued, I saw two other demons come in search of those two and asked them to be quick as their master (Satan) was waiting to receive the file. I could sense the desperate urgency within them for the given task fearing harsh repercussions.

Not completing a task successfully incites the wrath of Satan, and he disciplines his subjects in such a manner that even demons are scared of him. I saw those demons search for the file under the supervision of two other demons and finally, as they found the mentioned file, I could see the crease of worry leave their faces as they made their way to Satan with the file.

Jesus told me that at times these demons do take the wrong files deliberately, particularly the files with similar names, since to search for the right file among the rest was a task in itself; especially considering that these files belong to people around the world and there was no order in maintaining these files.

Hence, they pick up files with similar names (that explained the overwritings and striking out details, in an attempt to cover up) and make their way to Satan in the hope that he would not find out. When Satan does find out, he disciplines the particular demon responsible for the mistake and sends them back with a warning to come back with the right file.

As Jesus explained this to me, I saw a powerful demon enter this chamber with two others. This demon appeared to be holding a list of names and gave instructions to the other two based on this list. I understood that these instructions were in regard to the files. Jesus explained to me that this demon had the list of names of people who were going to be dead soon and arrive in hell shortly. He was giving instructions to the other two demons to keep their files ready in case Satan asked to see their files.

I assumed that this demon who held the list of names ruled this department, but Jesus told me that Satan himself rules this department. He said this, much to my astonishment, since I did not see Satan even once in this chamber. As a result my mind questioned, to which Jesus replied, "Daughter, Satan is not omnipresent. He does come here as and when he feels the need to from time to time. And whenever he comes he goes through the two sets of piles of files set on his table."

So that was his table. But I wondered why Satan should go through the two sets of piles of files on each time of his visit. Jesus said, "Daughter, he feels elated to see that those who have come back to him are much more in number than the ones who have abandoned him. Also, he tries his best to get back those who have abandoned him and he does so with vengeance."

Just then I saw Satan enter this chamber with hordes of demons. I could see that one in this group of demons who entered this chamber along with Satan carried Satan's thick black book—his record book—and another carried three new files. Satan entered the chamber amidst the chanting that he was lord. I could see Satan's love to be worshipped and praised. He straightaway rushed to the table where the two piles of files were assembled. He asked for his record book and checked the details of those who had come back to him. He looked seemingly pleased with the latest additions and uttered, "More, more." Then I saw him pick the three mentioned files of the ones who had come back to him from the small pile of files. While he did so, I saw the demon that carried the new files placing them on the table. Then I saw Satan himself fill the details of those who had come back to him in the new files and added these to that huge pile of files on that table. He handed the three old files to another demon in his cortege who placed these files underneath that table. Then Satan turned his attention to the small pile of files of those who had abandoned him; and after a random review, much to my shock, picked out one of the tattered file and discarded it saying, "We lost him." Then, I saw him strike the name of the person to whom this file belonged in his record book. After this he handed over his record book to one of the demons in his train of attendants who surrounded him and left. As he left the chamber with his cortege of demons, these demons chanted again that Satan was lord. Jesus said to me that Satan was on his way to earth.

It appeared that he had entered this chamber only to go through the files of the living on his table. I could see that the files on the table were maintained by Satan himself and that he was very focused in his goals and was working very hard to get souls for himself. This battle with the enemy is so real. Beloved, Satan is not relaxing. He is working hard to achieve his goals.

I could deduce from his maintenance of those files on his table (as he added those details himself in the new files and also struck out the name of the one individual) that he did not trust any of his demons when it came to souls. I also wondered why Satan should discard the tattered file that he had maintained over the years and said, "We lost him." Jesus answered, saying, "Daughter, it is only because the person just died." The realization that statement brought with itself opened my eyes to a new spiritual dimension.

Beloved, Satan does not consider any person lost even if they have abandoned him. He does not give up on them as long as they are alive. He hopes to get them back someday by his continual attempts. It is only with the death of the person that he really considers them lost, not otherwise. I watched him strike out the name of the person in his record book only with the person's death. This is why the Word of God teaches us to endure till the end: "He who endures to the end will be saved" (Matt. 24:13).

Beloved, you might be born again but Satan has not given up on you. As long as you are alive, he will try his best to get you back on his side.

Christians, are you listening? If we could be that focused in our goals, stop relaxing, and get as busy as the enemy for God and His work, I am sure we would make a big difference in this world.

I had wanted to know why the demons were so disorganized in maintaining the files in this chamber since I have seen them very organized in their attacks against Christians. After all, it would take them just a short time to arrange the files. They appeared to be so lethargic in not doing so. And also, if they do come to know prior to the death of those who belong to them, why then do they still hunt for those files once those souls arrive in hell? I found their lethargic nature in regard to maintaining files and the factual inaccuracies mentioned therein much similar to the running of a corrupt office in the world. Now I understood why this was so. These demons know that all information in regard to souls is maintained by Satan already in his record book, so they do not really care much about maintaining these files. Meanwhile, though Satan maintains his own record book, he compels those demons to maintain these files to ensure that they work hard. That explained the demons' annoyance and recklessness in maintenance of files.

Then Jesus looked at me and said, "Daughter, I have shown you the hidden activities of the enemy. Warn My people to continue steadfastly in prayer, being watchful in it (Col. 4:2). Let them be doers of the Word, not hearers only (James 1:22); only then can the arrows of the enemy be quenched (Eph. 6:16)."

Beloved, I have seen the enemy's seriousness in his war against God and His people. Satan and his demons' sole focus is on this battle. It is of crucial importance to understand his strategies in spiritual maturity and be prepared in alertness and equipped effectively in God's armor to be victorious against him.

It is evident from his diverse and dark activities that he plans and coordinates these personal attacks against Christians through his vast network of demons devoted to specific tasks.

Dear reader, I witnessed the reality of the adversary, Satan, and his invisible evil kingdom. This battle is very real as mentioned in the Bible.

> For we do not wrestle against flesh and blood, but against principalities, against powers, against the rulers of the darkness of this age, against spiritual hosts of wickedness in the heavenly places.
>
> —Ephesians 6:12

Satan employs different strategies in this battle to destroy one's Christian walk. Relying on his vast network of demons, Satan continually and desperately attempts to dethrone God and enthrone himself in the lives of those who belong to Christ. Every born-again Christian is continually involved in this spiritual warfare against such demonic attacks. His most severe attacks are directed at those uncompromising Christians who oppose him vehemently. These demonic attacks on a Christian can be physical, spiritual, emotional, or financial. The power of the enemy cannot be underestimated, yet at the same time not everything can be attributed to demonic attacks. It takes prayer and discernment to understand whether you are under such attacks. Satan is adept in influencing circumstances and to turn people against you to achieve his purposes. If you are not alert in this battle, you will perish by these arrows of the enemy.

> Be ye doers of the word, and not hearers only, deceiving your own selves.
>
> —James 1:22

Therefore,

> Put on the whole armor of God, that you may be able to
> stand against the wiles of the devil.
>
> —EPHESIANS 6:11

The enemy through his power does encourage and exploit evil desires and weaknesses of a mortal being. However, they do not make one commit sin, as I have mentioned before. Man is conceived in sin and because of this sinful nature a man or a woman commits sin of their own free will. Based on this free will, an individual has the choice to either resist or succumb to the temptation, and therefore is accountable to God for his or her actions.

God is calling for a spiritual awakening and maturity to understand the enemy's operating mechanism and thereby victoriously prevail against him.

As a wise Christian, you need to be prepared and vigilant of his attacks, which are very real dangers. The Bible warns of not giving place to the devil (Eph. 4:27). Knowingly participating in continual sinning provides the enemy an open doorway in your life.

Beloved, we can be victorious in this battle through Jesus Christ who has defeated the enemy: "Yet in all these things we are more than conquerors through Him who loved us" (Rom. 8:37).

Our Christian walk must be rooted in God's Word in righteousness and holiness for God's armor to be effective in our lives, without which we will be rendered powerless in front of a powerful enemy's effective schemes.

> Therefore lay aside all filthiness and overflow of wickedness,
> and receive with meekness the implanted word, which is
> able to save your souls.
>
> —JAMES 1:21

Chapter Eleven

LOST SOULS IN HELL

I am the Living One; I was dead, and behold, I am alive for ever and ever! And I hold the keys of death and Hades.

—REVELATION 1:18, NIV

PHARISEE

ONE EVENING IN 2001 Jesus appeared to me, came near, and said, "Daughter, come with Me." Instantly we were in a part of hell. The light that emanated from Jesus illuminated the place which otherwise was in pitch darkness. Through His light I could see that we stood outside a small black wooden door. Jesus looked at me and said, "Daughter, we are going inside this place."

With that, He began to walk, and I beside Him, right through the closed door and entered this place. I found this to be absolutely incredible and beyond belief to walk right inside through the closed door! My intellect and limited mindset expected Jesus to open the door to let us in, but He did not even touch the door nor require it to enter this place.

Here was Jesus in His greatness and majesty; the One who died and rose again with all authorities and powers made subject to Him; the Lord of both the dead and the living; the One who holds the keys of death and Hades; yet my futile mind had limited this great God.

He had surpassed my expectations yet again like before on countless occasions and proved He is God. It took a while to tune my limited self to the reality of an impossibility I had just experienced firsthand.

Why is it so difficult for a human mind to accept God just as He is? Why do we doubt and question His promises? Why do we negate and limit His powers when all that we need to do is trust and sit back in assurance that He is capable of taking care of everything. In fact, He is the answer to all our questions and the solution for our troubled souls.

His light illuminated my darkness, His very presence showed my imperfections; and I was ashamed of my inability to believe that He is capable of doing much and beyond my abilities, limitations, and thoughts. And I learned that with Jesus beside me, I can walk right through the closed door.

Reader, if you are waiting for God to open a closed door, let me tell you with Jesus next to you, you will walk right through that closed door. All that you need is Jesus beside you; His presence with you takes care of everything, including a closed door. Let us not limit Him in His capabilities and power, and let us give Him the glory due to Him.

As we entered this place, I could feel the slimy ground underneath and therefore treaded carefully. I could hear emphatic cries of a man coming from ahead of us. A dimly lit lantern hung in the corner of the entrance. In its reflection I could see that this was a dungeon. Huge bats hung and flew about. The place appeared to be in quietness except for the cries of the man and screeching of bats. We walked to the far end of the dungeon where I could see an isolated pit.

Jesus stopped in front of that isolated pit. It appeared to me that this place was specially assigned to this particular lost soul. I looked into this pit that appeared to be deep.

There was a blackened burned form of a man inside this pit, submerged in what appeared like fiery liquid. Though it appeared to be a liquid, flames of fire came out of it. The man seemed to be in a great torment. He wore an exquisite headdress that was very rich in appearance, an indication of his wealth and power while he was alive. What I found baffling was how and why the headdress was still intact. Why did the fire not destroy it?

Just then Jesus looked at me. He knew my thoughts and began to explain, "This is a soul of a Pharisee who lived at the time I was on earth. He was a witness to the miracles I performed. He saw Me drive out demons and raise the dead. He witnessed My death on the cross; and using his powers, he denounced My resurrection. He rejected Me as the Son of God though he was given plenteous opportunities to be saved. He was arrogant and proud of his beliefs and traditions, which he followed ardently, and he denied My work on the cross. He was not willing to come to Me and have life, which in My mercy I wanted him to receive. He had believed and prided in himself. Therefore, the headdress is a reflection of his identity, of what he lived and stood for, and is a constant reminder of his sin."

As we stood in front of this lost soul, he suddenly saw Jesus and pleaded, "Rabbi, I accept now that you truly are the Son of God. Have mercy get me out of this place."

This was a pitiful sight to behold. Jesus looked at him sorrowfully and said. "Now there is no hope. You rejected My salvation that was offered to you freely. If only you came to Me while alive, you would not be here today." Saying this, Jesus moved away from the pit and sorrowfully led me out of that eerie place.

> You have become estranged from Christ, you who attempt
> to be justified by law; you have fallen from grace.
>
> —GALATIANS 5:4

Beloved, are you estranged from Christ today as a result of that religious mindset like this Pharisee? It is time you set aside your false beliefs and pride. Come to Jesus in humility and accept His salvation plan. In doing so you receive His grace and the forgiveness of your sins.

WITCH

Again in 2001 I found myself standing beside Jesus in open ground in a part of hell. Jesus asked me to watch carefully as He told me that in that place, at times, Satan met those who belonged to him.

I could see that Satan was dressed in a black robe and in front of him was a thick black book. This was Satan's record book. It seemed that Satan was not aware of our presence. One soul had just arrived in hell. I could see that it was a soul of a woman. She was thrown in front of Satan by his demons. On seeing her there, he gave out a hearty laughter. He commanded his demons to bring the black book that was lying in front of him. I could see how much Satan likes to be served. That book was lying right in front of him and all that was required of him was to pick it up, yet he commanded his demons to get it for him.

I stood close to Satan and saw him open this book. I could see that its pages were thick and it contained names of people in an alphabetical order from A to Z. After flipping a few pages, he came to the letter with which her name started and found her name underneath that particular letter. I was surprised to see that next to her name was her complete address including the state and country she belonged to. Right underneath her address was marked WITCHCRAFT in big, bold, red letters. She had played a major role in witchcraft for Satan, brought him many souls, and also harmed many Christians.

Next to this was a complete list of other sins that she had committed while on earth. I read a few—adultery, incest, murder. The woman now seemed to be fearful of Satan whom she had served gladly while she was on earth. She had believed fervently in reincarnation after death; but she was brought to hell instead. Satan looked at her and said with authority, "You are mine." As soon as he said that, his demons came to get her.

As I watched, I saw her plead for death. She remembered the lady who shared about forgiveness of sins available to all those who came to Jesus Christ. Instead of accepting the offer of salvation, she had always argued against this and was convinced of her own beliefs. Remorseful now, this woman lamented, "That woman was right about Jesus, but I was deceived and refused to accept the truth." Then, she cried out with all her might, "Jesus, save me!" As soon as she uttered the name Jesus, the demons kicked her and she began to writhe in pain. I saw a demon thrust a dagger in her body and then she cried out more than before. The demons laughed and mocked her saying, "Bad for you! You did not accept what was offered to you; now you will be with us."

Then these two demons hacked her body in bits. I watched in horror. The woman's vociferous screams added to the fear so thick in the gloomy air. She begged and pleaded and suddenly shouted, "I want to die!" Hearing that, Satan and his demons laughed hysterically. As those demons came to get her, all pieces of her body came together. I saw demons drag her to what appeared like a cage that was prepared especially for her.

As soon as she entered that cage, I saw it light up in fire. I saw her engulfed by the fire and the woman screamed in great torment. As the fire subsided, I could see that all that remained was her blackened burned form. I heard her curse herself repeatedly for having rejected the good news of salvation in Jesus Christ.

I could not understand the bits of flesh that hung on the horizontal bars of her cage that were not destroyed by fire. Unable to comprehend what they meant, I asked Jesus about this. He explained to me, "Each bit of flesh represents a human sacrifice she offered for Satan in witchcraft." These bits of flesh served as a constant reminder of the murders she had committed on earth.

The Bible says, "I will destroy your witchcraft" (Mic. 5:12, NIV). It also tells us:

> The acts of the flesh are obvious:…witchcraft…and such
> like: of the which I tell you before, as I have also told you in

time past, that they which do such things shall not inherit the kingdom of God.

—GALATIANS 5:19–21, NIV

If you practice witchcraft in any form, please repent. You might be involved in white magic and consider yourself to be a good witch and believe that you are doing good to people, but you are being deceived by the lies of the enemy. Indulging in witchcraft, whether white or black, is a sin and this is an abomination to God. Please repent of your sin now while you have time, for after death it will be too late.

You might consider yourself to be a Christian and still practice witchcraft. Beloved, get rid of this duplicity and get right with God.

WIZARD

Another time in 2001 I witnessed another lost soul been brought to hell by two demons. Its appearance was that of a man. Jesus told me that this soul had practiced witchcraft while alive. This soul had been very confident that death would not come to him so soon. When he had least expected it, death struck him.

I could see that this soul was very angry with those demons as they controlled and ordered him about. While alive, he was deceived into believing that he had control over these demons. I watched in horror as I saw those demons pierce the lost soul's tongue with what appeared like countless sharp needles. As he screamed, the demons laughed. I could not understand why he was being tormented in his tongue. Jesus explained to me, "Daughter, he confessed his sins once when he came to Me but then he went back to Satan. Hence, the enemy's fury is great upon him for he acknowledged Me once with his tongue."

After the mentioned torment, I saw this lost soul taken by force to what looked like a cave. I could see an underground lake that flowed right through this cave. I saw this in the reflection of a dimly lit lantern that hung there inside the cave. The demons threw this lost soul in this lake; he instantly started to scream. This was a fiery lake, and I could see that this lost soul tried his best to get out of it.

After a while I saw them let this lost soul out of this lake. He then resembled a black burned skeleton. Everything about him seemed to have been eaten by this fiery lake including his eyes, yet he saw everything and experienced everything that was happening to him. He was very much alive though dead.

Those demons led him outside the cave and set him forcibly on what appeared like a black wooden sled. This sled had sharp arrows placed on both sides; each movement of the sled resulted in him being pierced by these sharp arrows. Agonized, he cried out for mercy. I watched in bewilderment as this lost soul was in a skeleton form yet he experienced the sharp pain caused by those arrows. He begged the demons to stop but there was no mercy and no respite to the horror.

As we continued to watch, I saw this bloodied lost soul pulled out of the torture sled and forced inside a white coffin. I could see sharp metal spikes all over the inside of this coffin. As I wondered about this white coffin, Jesus read my thoughts and said, "Daughter, white represents salvation and coffin represents death. This is in mockery to this man since he came to Me once and became My child but went back to witchcraft."

I saw those demons close the coffin. This lost soul's high-pitched screams of torment were heartrending. As soon as they closed the coffin, they threw it in the furnace of fire. I saw Jesus weep. He said to me, "Satan's fury is great upon those souls who once accepted Me but went back to him. These souls are tormented much more."

I could hear and see those demons laugh over this soul's pitiful cries. With that, I found myself back on earth. Jesus said, "My daughter, I will show you much more. Tell My children to be faithful and to endure till the end. 'He who endures till the end will be saved' (Matt. 10:22)."

Beloved, no matter what reason you have strayed away from

Jesus, come back to Him. Repent and He will forgive you. Please do not depart from this world without getting right with God.

DRUNKARD

At another time in 2001, suddenly Jesus appeared and instantly I found myself at what Jesus referred to as the entrance of hell. As I stood beside Jesus near the entrance of hell, I could see a lost soul arrive, escorted by two small-sized demons. Looking at him, Jesus said, "This soul, when alive, was a drunkard. Drinking liquor had been his one and only love. He never bothered to think what would happen if he died suddenly. His motto in life was: "I will live my life as I please. Who cares about death?"

This lost soul appeared to be fearful and horrified to arrive in hell. Instantly he was reminded of an evangelist who had constantly shared the good news of salvation in Jesus Christ with him and also warned him about hell. Now this lost soul cursed himself for not paying heed to the warning of the evangelist.

Suddenly he saw Jesus. He began to cry, "Jesus, I accept You now. Please forgive me!" At this, one of the demons who accompanied him kicked and scorned him saying, "It is too late for that now; this is your condemnation." Apparently these demons could not see Jesus and me.

We watched as this soul was taken to another part in hell where there was a large open ground and that seemed to be divided into several compartments. After walking a rough pathway for some time, we reached this place. As we approached, heartrending cries and painful screams accompanied with the awful stench of burning human flesh filled the dense air.

If not for Jesus, I would have never stepped into this ghastly place. I saw many demons outside these compartments wait in anticipation to be summoned. Jesus told me that these demons were specially assigned to this place and that they served as extras.

I wondered within myself at the nature of the torment that required their help as extras.

As we entered this compartment, I could see surge of fire emanate from several huge pots that seemed to be placed on fiery open pits. Also, there were several empty bottles lying about the place. I wondered what purpose those bottles served. Once they were inside the compartment, the two demons who accompanied the lost soul summoned for an extra while they held the lost soul with force to prevent him from escaping. I could see the lost soul try with all his might to escape from that dreadful place; but he soon gave up, having realized that it was impossible to escape since the place was full of watchful demons.

The third demon, the one who was summoned as an extra, picked up one of the bottles that was lying around. Much to my amazement, he scooped up some of the fire from the pot and filled the bottle with fire. Then he proceeded to serve this fire in the bottle to the lost soul and commanded him to consume that fiery drink.

As expected, this lost soul refused to even put this bottle to his mouth. He put up a stiff resistance, but in vain, as these demons were much too powerful for him. Soon he was drinking fire; and in no time all that remained of him was a blackened burned skeleton form.

This fire seemed to have eaten off his flesh. He now held the empty bottle in his skeletal form, yet he saw everything and felt everything. In the place of his eyes now remained empty sockets, yet tears appeared and disappeared as he cried out in great pain. He begged those demons to stop the torment. I felt so sorry for him for it was terrible to see his transformation to this pathetic state.

Those demons mocked and scorned him saying, "You loved to drink; now enjoy this drink of fire." The empty bottle was quickly filled up with fire again, and he was made to consume another. This process of torment repeated itself endlessly.

This lost soul sobbed like a child and repeatedly cursed himself for having rejected the opportunity he had on earth to accept Jesus.

Meanwhile, the flames of fire in the pot continued to burn with much rage. I did not see the fire ever die down. Also, I wondered about those bottles that could withstand and did not crack under such high heat, unbearable by human standards. Yet the bottle remained intact. As I looked around, I saw many others like him in that place and a similar torment was meted out to each of them.

Jesus began to speak with sadness, "If only they had come to Me, they would not be here today. There are many souls here who thought they had time on their side to make a definite decision for Me. Alas, they left the world much before they had thought. Daughter, tell the people of the world not to wait till it is too late, for they do not know when death will strike them. I want to save everybody from this horrible place, but it is up to each of them to believe and accept My salvation plan that is offered freely. The blood that I shed on Calvary will wash all their sins. If they only ask Me, I will forgive them." The words of Jesus kept ringing in my ears from Matthew 9:6: "The Son of Man has authority on earth to forgive sins" (NIV).

Dear reader, are you waiting to receive Jesus as your Savior when you are old? Are you saying this to yourself, "I am young, why bother about God now?" You might not have time on your side. Life is uncertain, and you may not even make it to the end of this day. Death is an uninvited guest and comes knocking at your door when you least expect it.

Do not wait to make a definite decision for Jesus Christ when you are old, for it might be too late then. Be prepared now! For you do not know when death will strike you. The Bible says, "Drunkards will [not] inherit the kingdom of God" (1 Cor. 6:10).

If you are a drunkard, please repent and renounce your sin. The effect of liquor will wear off once you die, and you will wake up in all your senses to your condemnation. Perhaps you want to give up this addiction but find it difficult to do so. Jesus Christ offers you hope. If you ask and let Him set you free, you will be free indeed:

"Therefore if the Son makes you free, you shall be free indeed" (John 8:36).

Beloved, be filled with the Holy Spirit instead of being drunk, as the Word of God instructs us: "And do not be drunk with wine, in which is dissipation; but be filled with the Spirit" (Eph. 5:18).

MURDERER

> Murderers…shall have their part in the lake which burns
> with fire and brimstone, which is the second death.
> —REVELATION 21:8

Suddenly, again in 2001, I found myself beside Jesus in a part of hell where there were cells. Jesus held my hand. After passing several rows of cells, He stopped in front of a particular cell. I could see a lost soul in the form of a man inside this dingy cell. This lost soul seemed to hold a make-believe gun in his hand and pretended to shoot with it.

I could not understand what this soul was up to. In fact, I thought for a while that he was playing a game on his own, but I was baffled as to why this role-playing seemed to be non-stop.

Knowing my thoughts, Jesus began to explain to me, "This soul was a murderer and killed many with his gun. In death this action is a constant reminder of his sin."

Suddenly huge flames of fire lit up the cell and seemed to consume him. His desperate loud shouts and wails filled the place. Soon all that remained of him was a burned skeleton form, yet he was alive and not dead. At this point the lost soul suddenly appeared to see Jesus, and he cried in a loud voice, "Get me out of here! How long will I be tormented?"

With sadness, Jesus answered, "I wanted so much to save you from coming here. I sent many people to tell you about Me, but you did not listen to any of them. Finally I sent My dear child who shared with you about Me; but in anger you said to him, 'I do not believe in your God. And even if your God will send me to hell for shooting you dead, I do not care.' And with that you shot him dead. But before you could even move out of there, you were shot dead by your trusted, close friend. Now the judgment is set."

With that the lost soul began to cry the most piercing heart-rending cries that rang in my ears for a long time. In grief, Jesus walked away from this cell and gestured me to follow him.

Beloved, you might be a murderer and happen to read this book. You may or may not be caught for your crime in this world. You may think that nobody knows about it and you are safe. Remember, God knows about this murder you have committed and one day you will stand in front of this God who rules in righteousness and justice and you will give an account of this sin.

Please repent! Do not depart from this world without getting right with God. Jesus Christ will wash this stain of murder away if you just ask Him. There is no sin so big that He cannot pardon.

> "Come now, and let us reason together," says the LORD. "Though your sins are like scarlet, They shall be as white as snow; Though they are red as crimson, They shall be like wool."
>
> —ISAIAH 1:18

Come to Jesus Christ today.

ABORTIONISTS

Jesus and I again passed a series of cells and came to a particular cell. Jesus stopped there. I could see a lost soul of a man inside the cell. He appeared to be a doctor performing a make-believe abortion. Suddenly this scene changed and the fire swept over him. In the place of the doctor, now remained a burned skeleton form.

Jesus told me that this lost soul, when alive, was a doctor who did abortions willfully and knew what he was doing was sin. Nevertheless, that did not stop him from carrying out abortions.

Jesus went on to say, "I am the giver of life. Right from the time a child is conceived in the womb, it becomes a living soul. Whoever snuffs that life will not go unpunished. Abortion is a murder in my sight. I will punish the one who performs abortion and the one who undergoes the abortion. No man has any right to take away a life that has been given by Me. If he does, I will hold him guilty." Jesus spoke these words firmly with anger.

Suddenly the tormented soul saw Jesus and cried out to Him to get him out of there. Jesus looked at this lost soul sadly and walked past.

Grieved, we walked past rows of many cells. Finally Jesus turned to the right and stopped in front of a cell. I could see inside the cell a lost soul of an old woman with countless tiny skulls. Looking closely, I could see that she was weeping over those tiny skulls. Jesus explained to me that each skull represented the life she had aborted willfully on earth.

Flames of fire rose out of nowhere and engulfed her completely as I watched. Soon her shouts and screams for help turned to sobs and laments, "Why did I do these abortions?"

The skulls were a constant reminder of her sin and tormented her greatly. Jesus told me that, while alive, this woman was a nurse and that she has been here for a long time. She was now remorseful of her sin, but it was too late since judgment had set in. This lost soul was lost in her torment and not once did she look away from those skulls. Her sin was constantly before her and the very focus of her attention.

Sorrowfully, we moved away from that cell.

Then in July of 2012 I suddenly found myself beside Jesus standing in front of cells in a part of hell. We walked for a while, and then Jesus stopped in front of a cell.

I could see that inside the cell was the lost soul of a young teen-aged girl with a large blotch of blood in her abdomen area. I wondered what this teenager was doing there. She was the youngest so far that I had seen in hell. Jesus told me, "This young girl died while undergoing an abortion. The blotch represents this sin. She knew about Me, yet went away far from Me. I waited for her to return back to Me; instead she went further and further away from Me. She did not heed My call."

Suddenly this lost soul saw Jesus and began to cry pitifully, "Give me another chance. It is all my mother's fault. It is because of her that I am here. Why did she not discipline me so that I did not stray from You? Why did she let me do whatever I wanted? Punish her and get me out of here. Please! Please!"

Right at that moment, in front of us a fire started on the area where the blotch was and spread quickly enveloping her in its flames. She screamed in agonizing pain.

Sadly, as we left the place, Jesus spoke, "If only she had come back to Me, I would have forgiven her. There are many like her here. Warn the people of the world not to abort innocent lives."

With that statement, I found myself back on earth.

Beloved, please repent if you have participated in this sin: performed or undergone an abortion. Jesus terms it as murder. You might get away with this on earth, but you will not get away with it after death. Please repent! The blood of Jesus Christ can cleanse that stain of blood of the innocent life that you have aborted.

> "Come now, and let us reason together," says the LORD.
> "Though your sins are like scarlet, They shall be as white as
> snow; Though they are red as crimson, They shall be like
> wool."
>
> —ISAIAH 1:18

SUICIDES

In 2001, again I was translated in my spirit and found myself in a part of hell. I could see cells there. Jesus and I walked past several of these cells for a while. Jesus stopped in front of yet another cell. On top of the cell was written the number 29. I could see a soul of a young man inside the cell. He had a deep scar on his neck and there was a rope hanging in the inside of the cell.

This lost soul held the bar of the cell and repeatedly cursed himself. But I did not understand the relevance of the number 29 or his scar so evident in his neck, and also wondered about the rope in his cell.

As I stood perplexedly looking at this lost soul, Jesus began to explain to me the meanings behind what I saw that were otherwise impossible for me to ever understand.

Jesus said, "Daughter, this man committed suicide at the age of twenty-nine; hence, number 29 refers to the age of his death. The rope you see inside the cell was the means by which he hung himself to death and as a result left a deep scar on his neck."

I listened as this lost soul blamed and cursed his father and himself for this miserable state that he was in. He constantly questioned his act of suicide, "Why did I kill myself and end up in this place?"

Suddenly as I watched, huge flames of fire from nowhere started at the deep scar on his neck and spread throughout his form within no time. He was consumed in flames of fire. All that remained of him was a burned skeleton form but the scar still remained and so did the rope. The fire had spared these two as the mark of unrighteousness, and his sin was forever in front of him and tormented him. It appeared that he could not see Jesus or me and was lost in his own torment, which was so great.

As we moved away from this cell, sorrowfully Jesus said, "No man has any right to take away his life, since life is a gift given by Me."

Jesus asked me to follow Him and led me in front of a particular cell on top of which was written 18. This cell appeared to be a bit wider than the previous cell. I could see a lost soul of a young man who appeared to be in great agony and torment. He appeared to be confined to the ground, and I could see a demon next to him. I was shocked to see what this demon was doing to him.

I could see that this cell housed an open fiery pit and placed in this fiery pit were dozens of iron rods being heated. This demon was inflicting immense torture to this young man's soul by the means of these extremely hot iron rods. This lost soul screamed out loud; and though he seemed to be unable to move from his shoulder right up to his feet, he felt every torture inflicted to him. As I watched, great flames of fire arose from his shoulders, spread to his feet, and came back with a fury up to his head, covering his face and entire body in flames. Yet he did not make any attempt to get up.

Jesus told me that this lost soul had no mobility from his shoulders right through his feet while alive, and he had died in that state. Yet I could see that this lost soul experienced and felt every torturous pain that was inflicted to him in hell.

This lost soul cursed in anger as he found the torture unbearable. In spite of his pleadings to the demon to stop, his torments continued. I saw him beg for water to drink while the demon scorned him.

As we watched this entire episode with grief, Jesus began to speak, "This young man committed suicide at the age of eighteen years. This was his second attempt, and he was successful. When he attempted to kill himself the first time, I sent a young woman to share My love with him and saved him. He had been a drug addict from an early stage of his life. He started to experiment with his life, as he wanted to see how it would be to end his life. Soon he attempted to kill himself but did not succeed as I wanted to save him. This young man thought if he became a Christian, his life would become dull, so he turned Me aside. Drugs and the company of evil friends drove him to attempt suicide the second time, in which he succeeded. His friends made him believe that there was no hell, and urged him to live life to the optimum as he wanted to. After coming here, he was shocked to learn hell does exist and is a place of immense agony, pain, and torture. If only he had accepted Me as his Savior, I would have saved him and he would not be here in this place. He turned Me aside and has ended up here. He now regrets having missed that opportunity to accept Me when the young woman presented the gospel."

Soon Jesus and I walked past that cell in sadness.

People, please do not turn aside Jesus by walking in the ways of your heart, and in the sight of your eyes, but know that for all these God will bring you into judgment (Eccles. 11:9).

Beloved, there is a hell, as this young man found out too late after his departure from earth. Please do not try and experiment with death in any form, whether through drugs or suicide. Your life is a gift given of God, as Jesus said, and killing yourself will land you in hell.

> Don't you know that you yourselves are God's temple and that God's Spirit dwells in your midst? If anyone destroys God's temple, God will destroy that person.
> —1 Corinthians 3:16–17

Do not wait to accept Jesus Christ at a later date; do it now!

The age-old notion depicted in movies that lovers are together in death is far from the truth. Lovers, if you end your lives, not only will you be apart from each other but will also be in hell. I witnessed this truth in hell.

In 2012 I was instantly translated to a part of hell and found myself beside Jesus. We walked past several lost souls in cells. Jesus stopped in front of a particular cell where I beheld a lost soul of a young woman aged nineteen. She was cursing her lover for her state of torment in hell. I heard her say, "If not for..., I would not be here. It is his fault; it was his idea."

I could see that she was lost in her own torment, which was so great. Jesus told me that she had shot herself, as she and her lover, in a bid to end their lives, believed that as lovers they would be together after death.

Instead they ended up in hell and apart. And also, there was no possibility of ever seeing each other again. Moreover, they now cursed each other for their state of torment.

This lost soul did not appear to see us. She appeared to be holding a make-believe pistol in her hand and shooting herself. Over and over again, she would enact the scene of her killing. Suddenly fire from nowhere started at her hands and enveloped her completely in its flames. Her pitiful screams filled the place. Then the fire appeared to subside. Now all that remained of her was burned skeleton form, yet she continued to enact the scene of her killing. The act of torment continued to repeat itself, over which she had absolutely no control. This was her wage of unrighteousness and a constant reminder of her sin.

Jesus said sadly as we moved past that cell, "This woman was given many opportunities, but she brushed away each opportunity and said, 'How do I know whether Jesus is for real? I am young and want to live my life as I want.'"

We walked for a while again and passed several other cells. Jesus stopped in front of yet another cell. I could see a lost soul of a young man aged nineteen, which I could make out from the digits on top of this cell. This lost soul seemed to be holding an imaginary pistol in his hand and shot himself similar to the previous lost soul. The fire from nowhere started at his hands and enveloped him completely in its flames, and his terrifying screams filled the place. Then the fire appeared to subside. Now he was a burned skeleton form. Yet he continued to enact the same scene of his killing similar to the previous lost soul. The act of torment continued to repeat itself, over which he had no control.

Jesus said to me, "This lost soul was the young woman's lover." As we watched, he kept saying, "I am tired of all this. If not for that woman, I would not be here today. It is all her fault." With that, he cursed her for his state of continual torment.

Beloved, if you kill yourself, you will land up in hell where the torment never ends. Please listen to me; please do not attempt to take your own life. Death is not to be experimented with. I witnessed these souls languishing in hell because they ended their lives.

I heard a saying several years back that if somebody were to commit suicide at an age earlier than the age they were to die that the soul roams the earth for the remaining years till the actual age set for their death. For example, if somebody's actual age to depart from this earth is fifty but he committed suicide at twenty-five, for twenty-five years his soul would continue to roam the earth. I found this saying far from the truth. The Bible says after death is the judgment (Heb. 9:27). I found this to be the absolute truth, even if someone were to take his or her own life. So please follow the Word of God and do not experiment with death.

Suicide is not a quick fix solution. It will land you instantly in hell in eternal torment. I sincerely pray that you will give Jesus a chance and turn to Him rather than resorting to this pathway to hell. You might be facing problems and difficulties in life that nobody can solve; please come to Jesus, for He will solve those problems.

IDOL WORSHIPPERS

> Do not be deceived…idolaters…will [not] inherit the kingdom of God.
>
> —1 CORINTHIANS 6:9–10

At another time in 2001, again I was instantly translated to a part of hell and found myself in front of yet another cell. This cell was very small. I could see a lost soul of a man languishing in much torment inside this cell.

Jesus said to me, "Daughter, while alive, this man was an idol worshipper and believed firmly that I am just *one* among many gods. With this in mind, he never really bothered to accept Me as the way, the truth, and the life. He did not believe in the forgiveness of sins offered by Me but instead believed in reincarnation. His life ended in grief. And much to his shock, he was brought here."

This lost soul appeared to be engrossed with his head focused down. I wondered why, and then I saw where his attention was. He was intently watching the fire that had started from nowhere in the center of the cell and spread engulfing the entire cell in flames. His helpless shouts turned to groans, and the soul waited in fear as the fire appeared to die down then would suddenly come back with rage. This process of torment was unending, and he was lost in his torment and never once looked up.

My heart cried to see his pitiful state, and I turned to Jesus. He said sadly, "I gave him a chance to repent, but he turned down that chance. Now the judgment is set. It is too late; too late." Saying so, Jesus led me away from that cell.

He asked me to follow Him, and we walked for a while. If not for the grace of God, I would have never been able to walk that difficult pathway. Jesus held my hand and helped me walk until we entered another place. My mind could not comprehend what I saw.

I saw surge of huge flames of fire come out of huge pots. It was a large open space that contained many such huge pots. Many demons moved about this place and supervised the torment meted out to the condemned.

I beheld a lost soul of a woman who appeared to be middle aged. I could see her inside of one such huge fiery pot that burned with much rage. Her torment was continual, despite her pleadings. Her shouts of despair added to the cries of the dead yet living who were there. This was accompanied with the nauseating stench of burning flesh.

Jesus said to me, "This woman, while alive, willfully remained an idol worshipper though her neighbor lovingly shared about Me many times. She rejected Me and also turned as an enemy of Me. She prevented many people from coming to Me. Now, after coming here, she acknowledges Me and that she was wrong; but now it's too late." With that, Jesus led me out of that place and I found myself back on earth.

Beloved, worship of idols is demon worship. Repent now and come to Jesus.

RICH AND FAMOUS (1900–2000)

Again in 2001 Jesus came to me and said, "Daughter, come with Me. I want to show you some other parts in hell." He held my hand and I instantly found us in front of a black door. I could see that a dimly lit lantern hung above the door to guide the path.

Jesus asked me to read what was written on top of this door. I read what it said: "The Rich and Famous (1900–2000)." Jesus told me that the very rich and famous of the world who died during the period 1900–2000 were found here. Also all the lost souls present here had known about Him but refused to acknowledge and accept Him in their lives.

He asked me to follow Him. We went through the closed door right inside. It was a huge open place and appeared to be lit up in fire. I could see that this place contained cells as well as open fiery pits.

A Princess

As we stood there, Jesus said, "Look there," and pointed to a particular lost soul of a woman. I recognized her as a famous princess known for her beauty. Instantly her form changed to a blackened burned skeleton. She was neither in a cell or a pit; instead she was chased by four demons with spears that were tormenting her. She pleaded for them to stop the torment while they scoffed at her. Her cries were so pathetic and painful.

Though she had a good stature while alive, she appeared so helpless in front of those demons. She was trying her best to run away from them but could not. I pitied to see this princess hounded and tormented by those evil beings.

Jesus went on to say, "While alive, she never bothered to share any relationship with Me. I was immaterial and nonexistent for her. She sought and went after all kinds of sensual pleasures and sinned in My sight. Death came to her when she least expected it. She was horrified to reach here and realize that this was her eternal condemnation. She knew what My Word said about hell, yet never bothered to believe or accept it. Now she constantly regrets her sinful life on earth and having missed the opportunity to accept Me."

Prime Ministers

With that, Jesus began to walk toward the cells holding my hand. He stopped in front of a cell and asked me to look inside this cell. I saw a famous prime minister of a nation. He was inside this cell and appeared exactly the same as while alive on earth.

Jesus said, "This prime minister, while alive, did not believe that I am *the* way but was convinced that I am *one* of the ways. Many dignitaries told him about Me, but he argued with them all and even tried to convince them of his own beliefs. After coming here, he realized that he had made a big mistake, and since then is in constant torment."

I saw the lost soul of the prime minister light up in flames of fire and change to a blackened burned skeleton form and then come back to the way he looked on earth.

Then Jesus and I crossed to the other side where the pits were. We began to walk near the fiery pits. Jesus stopped right in front of two pits and showed me two more prime ministers.

I could see that they were burning in open fiery pits and one of them appeared as a mass of blood. To my amazement he continued to burn in that state. It was a ghastly sight to behold. Jesus explained to me that this prime minister, while alive, had taken many lives on earth and the blood of all those lives were upon him.

Presidents

Then Jesus moved on to another pit and asked me to look into this pit that burned with raging fire. I recognized this lost soul as a famous president of a powerful nation. Jesus told me that, while alive, this president had never cared to give Him a thought. His life was all about drinking and indulging in sinful pastimes. After his death he realized that he had made a terrible mistake.

This lost soul of the president was in deep torment. He seemed to be lost in his torment. I could see the flames of fire become fiercer each time.

Jesus stopped by another pit and asked me to see below. In that pit, I saw another famous president of the same powerful nation. I could see that he was burning in raging flames of fire. I also noticed a thick black chain around him that was not destroyed by fire.

Jesus explained to me that this president was set free once from his sins but went back to the bondage of sin and died in that state. The chain indicated his bondage. I felt so sorry to see this once famous president lament and weep in deep torment. He did not seem to notice us and was lost in his own torment.

Social Worker

A little further away from this pit was another open fiery pit. Jesus stopped in front of this pit and asked me to look into this pit. As I looked below, I could see a lost soul of a woman known for her charitable deeds. I was shocked to see her there burning in flames of fire. She was in deep torment. She appeared to see Jesus. Jesus looked at her and said, "Woman, your righteous deeds are like filthy rags (Isa. 64:6). You knew that without Me, you cannot enter heaven, but still you refused to acknowledge Me. This is your eternal death."

Jesus held my hand and as I walked carefully in between the pits. I could see many fiery open pits in that place.

King

As we began to walk past those pits, I heard the moaning cries of a man from a nearby pit saying, "I was a king. I was a king." This lost soul saw Jesus and said with much remorse, "I did not acknowledge You as the King of kings. Please forgive me and get me out of here. I have been here so long; please get me out." Jesus did not say a word. As we walked past that pit, He said, "This lost soul was the king of a powerful nation."

Reader, Jesus Christ is the King of kings; acknowledge Him as such. Do not be like this king who realized this truth after his death.

Queen

As we walked past that pit, I heard the moaning cries of a woman who was burning in the nearby pit. I asked Jesus about this lost soul of a woman. He said to me "While alive, she was queen of a rich nation. She was placed in an authoritative position, yet she never acknowledged Me or told others about Me." It was pitiful to behold her suffer in hell, much in contrast to her earlier life of luxury on earth.

Jesus did not stop in front of any of them. He said to me, "Let this be a warning to the world."

You might be a king, a queen, a princess, a president, or prime minister or even be known exclusively for your charitable deeds. Let me warn you; if you do not have Jesus Christ in your life as your Savior, you are just a step away from hell. Without Jesus, everything is meaningless, including the titles that might be attached to your name in this world, your massive wealth, your beauty, your fame, etc. Without being washed in His blood, you are doomed. Your title, position, charitable acts, wealth, or fame will not take you to heaven. Please repent and acknowledge, in humility, the need to be saved in the name of Jesus and be born again.

After death you will be stripped of everything you held dear or valued or were proud about on earth. You will fall under one of the categories: either lost or saved. Your titles, status, richness, or the self-righteous acts of charity will become immaterial. "For what is a man profited, if he shall gain the whole world, and lose His own soul?" (Matt. 16:26).

Your self-righteous acts do not earn you salvation. In His mercy, God saves us "not by works of righteousness which we have done, but according to His mercy He saved us, through the washing of regeneration and renewing of the Holy Spirit" (Titus 3:5).

Give Jesus the honor due to His name and accept Him as your Savior.

> And I will say to my soul, "Soul, you have many goods laid up for many years; take your ease; eat, drink, and be merry." But God said to him, "Fool! This night your soul will be required of you; then whose will those things be which you have provided?" So is he who lays up treasure for himself, and is not rich toward God.
>
> —LUKE 12:19–21

MAGICIANS (1900–2000)

> But the...sorcerers...shall have their part in the lake which burns with fire and brimstone, which is the second death.
>
> —REVELATION 21:8

Jesus took my hand; and after passing through those pits, I was relieved to come out of the black door. Jesus looked at me and said, "There is something else I want to show you."

With that I saw a staircase ahead of us. We climbed up the staircase. The stairs were wooden and black in color. Through the light of Jesus, I could see in that place of utter darkness.

We came in front of yet another closed black door. On top of the door was written "The Magicians (1900–2000)." Jesus said to me, "The magicians across the world who made pacts with Satan and died during this period are found here. Some of them were very popular and known across the globe."

We stood outside the black door; I could feel the intensity of the heat of the place from outside the door. As we walked through the door, the heat tremendously increased. I could see that it was a much bigger place than the rich and the famous, and I soon found out that the torment here was also much higher.

I saw many lost souls of magicians here in great torment. Jesus said, "These magicians had made a pact with Satan and served him wholeheartedly while alive. They offered regular sacrifices to him. In this manner they obtained favors from Satan, performed those feats, and had everything they craved for in the world. Their torment is much more for having lived for and sold their souls to Satan."

> And the devil said to Him, "All this authority I will give You, and their glory; for this has been delivered to me, and I give it to whomever I wish."
>
> —LUKE 4:6

Saying this, Jesus stopped in front of a cell that appeared larger than what I had come across before in hell. Jesus pointed to the name of the magician written on top of the cell. I read the name of the magician; he was a world-renowned magician. I was appalled to see the torment meted out. This is what I saw: the parts of his spirit body were segregated from each other. One demon was specially assigned for his torture. I could see within this cell sharp knives, blades, and iron bars placed in a pot and heated over the fiery pit. These were readied to mete out the horrendous torture to the lost soul. I then saw the demon inflict gruesome torture to each part of his spirit body with these extremely hot sharp knives, blades, and iron bars.

The magician's agonizing cries were heartrending, and the horrible stench of burning flesh filled the place. It appeared as if each part of the magician cried out to stop the gruesome endless torment.

With sadness, we moved away from this cell of the once world-famous magician to another cell. Jesus stopped in front of another cell that was almost opposite to the previous one. I could see the occupant magician's name written on top of the cell.

Jesus said, "The previous lost soul you just witnessed considered this magician to be his role model and walked in his footsteps. This magician was a globally renowned magician and much more popular than the other magician. In his time, he was very well-known for his feats."

This cell was bigger than the previous cell. There were two demons especially assigned to this lost soul's torture. The cruel torture meted out to this soul was much worse than the previous one. Each bone in his spirit body was separated and subjected to horrible torture. I simply cannot describe his horrendous screams that accompanied each separation.

As I beheld in horror, I could see his fingers, which lay in the corner within the cell, and one of the two demons specially assigned to his torture seriously engaged in separating the bones of these fingers. It was a ghastly sight, yet awfully real. I watched the other demon heat the iron rods, knives, and sharp blades to mete out the dreadful torture in a similar fashion as the previous magician.

As I watched in horror, all of the magician's bones were subjected to abject torment with the help of these extremely hot iron rods, knives, and sharp blades. His bloodcurdling cries became much more intense. He felt every cruel torture he was subjected to, and it appeared as if each of his bones cried out, "No! No!" This torment was unending with no respite.

Jesus said to me with sadness, "The magicians will have their part in the lake of fire. Warn the magicians before it is too late," and He led me out of that place.

The cruel torture and pathetic cries of the magicians, along with the revolting stench of burning flesh, lingered on my mind for a very long time. Magicians, please repent! These two lost souls were very well-known magicians, and I was shown these things to warn you. The Bible warns against practicing magic arts. I may not know you, yet I do not want you to go there to hell where your torment will be never ending. Your pact with Satan can be broken in Jesus' name. Please repent and come to Jesus now. You may be a magician and may not have made a pact with Satan; nevertheless, please repent and renounce this sin. It is an abomination to God.

As Jesus led me out of that place and we walked on a narrow

pathway, I saw two demons and they saw me too. They said to one another, "Catch her!" It was then that I realized that I was alone. I cried out in panic, "Jesus, where are You?" I started to run with all my might and reached for the door that was ahead of me. The door opened for me and shut promptly after me, much to my relief. Suddenly Jesus appeared. I asked Him, "Lord, why did You leave me alone?" He replied, "Daughter, I will never leave you nor forsake you (Heb. 13:5). I have been with you all the time and I brought you out of that door [now I understood why the door opened and shut promptly]. I became invisible to make you understand how a lost soul feels in hell. I have shown you all these parts of hell to warn the people of the world not to come here. Unless they accept Me as their Savior and live a life approved of Me, there is no escape. I am the way, the truth, and the life" (John 14:6).

Saying thus, Jesus held my hand and brought me back.

CATHOLICS

In 2005 I found myself standing next to Jesus near the entrance of hell. At that moment I saw a lost soul of an aged woman being dragged by two demons. She appeared to be arguing with them while they asked her to shut up. Jesus told me that this woman, while alive, was a worshipper of Mary.

I watched as she began to cry out loud and said, "I argued with everyone who shared with me the salvation offered by Jesus. I was confident and proud of my faith passed down to me through my parents. I had believed with all my heart that what I practiced was the absolute truth. I have made a terrible, terrible mistake."

As she spoke those words, the demons laughed. I saw her being taken to a cell and thrown inside. As soon as she was thrown inside, the fire seemed to arise from nowhere and enveloped her in its raging flames. She cried for mercy and asked for death. I heard her lament for missing the many opportunities she was given on earth to be saved. She now realized that without Jesus, it was impossible to enter heaven. Now, as she resembled a blackened burned skeleton, she wailed and cursed herself for her state.

Beloved, do not be like this soul who found it too late to realize that Jesus Christ alone takes you to heaven. Mary, like any other mortal being, was conceived in sin and needed the blood of Jesus to cleanse her of her sins to be saved. If you happen to worship her or the saints, you are an idol worshipper. You need to repent of this sin to go to heaven.

Jesus Christ was conceived through the Holy Spirit and not in sin, unlike any man. He became sin for us that we might become the righteousness of God in Him: "For He made Him who knew no sin to be sin for us, that we might become the righteousness of God in Him" (2 Cor. 5:21).

If you are praying to Mary and the saints, you are deceived by the enemy and are opening yourself to demons. Beloved, Mary and the saints cannot wash your sins and answer your prayers since they were mortal beings. There is no other name given other than Jesus Christ who can save: "Nor is there salvation in any other, for there is no other name under heaven given among men by which we must be saved" (Acts 4:12).

Please repent now and be washed in the blood of Jesus Christ.

Jesus and I walked away in much sadness from this cell. He led me to the corner where there was a cluster of cells put together. He said, "Daughter, the occupants of these cells, while alive, were worshippers of Mary. They knew about Me, yet they rejected Me." Saying this, Jesus stopped there and asked me to watch carefully.

Suddenly I saw Satan appear. He did not appear to see us and entered this place. Right in front of our eyes, as soon as he entered the place, I saw his form change to Mary. He commanded worship by saying, "Worship me; worship me." The inhabitants of these cells bowed their heads in worship in fear of Satan.

All the lost souls inside this place, in their blackened burned skeleton forms, chanted, "Hail Mary! Hail Mary!" in fear of Satan. Amidst their chants, I saw flames of fire light up these cells. Satan, nevertheless, forced them to keep chanting this, though they were enveloped in flames of fire. Amidst their agonizing torment, they dared not stop chanting, for Satan commanded worship.

While alive, these lost souls by their free will had chosen to worship Mary and had rejected the Savior, being deceived by Satan. After their death and in hell, they were forced to continue, even though they knew now that in worshipping Mary, they had been worshipping Satan himself.

Beloved, beware of idol worship in any form. For idol worship is worship of Satan and his demons. If your worship is not directed toward Jesus, it is automatically directed to the adversary. The Bible says that there is no other name than Jesus who can save you and therefore He alone must be worshipped. If you are worshipping any other name, whoever it might be, you are worshipping Satan himself. Satan does everything in his power to be worshipped. The Bible mentions in Luke that Satan tempted Jesus by offering Him everything in his power in exchange for worship.

> And the devil said to Him, "All this authority I will give You, and their glory; for this has been delivered to me, and I give it to whomever I wish. Therefore, if You will worship before me, all will be Yours."
>
> —Luke 4:6–7

Repent now and escape hell.

Muslim

Jesus led me away from that place. After crossing several other cells, He stopped in front of yet another cell. I could see a lost soul of a woman inside this cell. She appeared to be clad in a black burqa. As I watched, her form changed to a burned skeleton form.

Jesus told me that, while alive, she was a Muslim and had practiced her faith ardently. She died as a result of a sudden illness.

After her death she was brought here, and since then has been in great torment.

I could see that she was lame in her right leg. As I stood outside this cell and watched her, she saw me, and said, "I thought Jesus was a prophet and not the Son of God. I never accepted His salvation plan and am suffering in hell. Please warn the Muslims and tell them not to come here."

Reader, if you are a Muslim and reading this book, this is not by chance. Jesus is the Son of God; and without accepting Him as a Savior in your life, you will end up in hell. Do not pass from this life without accepting Jesus Christ.

> For God so loved the world that He gave His only begotten Son, that whoever believes in Him should not perish but have everlasting life.
>
> —JOHN 3:16

UNBELIEVER

> But the…unbelieving…shall all have their part in the lake which burns with fire and brimstone, which is the second death.
>
> —REVELATION 21:8

In 2007 Jesus held my hand and brought me to a part of hell where I saw a lost soul of a man hung upside down on a cross. I was bewildered to see this soul in such a state. The man saw Jesus and began begging earnestly, "Please get me out of here. I accept now that you are the Son of God and not just a good man."

Jesus began to speak to me, "Daughter, this man, while alive, denied that salvation comes through My blood shed on the cross for sins. This soul convinced himself that I am not a Savior but a good man. Since he rejected salvation, his punishment is a constant reminder of the sinful state he died in."

> The wages of sin is death, but the gift of God is eternal life in Christ Jesus our Lord.
>
> —ROMANS 6:23

Jesus continued, "Now it is too late. There are so many people on earth who deny that I am the way, the truth, and the life and say that I am a good man and not Savior."

> This is good and acceptable in the sight of God our Savior, who desires all men to be saved and to come to the knowledge of the truth. For there is one God and one Mediator between God and men, the Man Christ Jesus, who gave Himself a ransom for all, to be testified in due time.
>
> —1 TIMOTHY 2:3–6

SEXUALLY IMMORAL

In 2008 I was instantly translated to a part of hell where I could see a sea of men and women in their blackened skeleton forms lined in queues. No matter how much I tried, I could not see where the queue ended. Instead I could see lost souls added constantly to the queue. Deafening screams of terror and nauseating stench of burning flesh filled the choking air. This was a never-ending human chain, and it appeared that each soul was lost in his or her torment and oblivious of the presence of others.

Jesus told me that these were the souls of sexually immoral and were ready to be cast into the lake of fire (Rev. 21:8).

The demons were present there in several forms, but no matter what form they took, they continued to inflict the torment with spears.

What amazed me was that though they were all blackened burned skeleton forms, the particular area of origin of their sin was singled out, highlighted, and subjected to continual torment. In fact, the torment started from the area highlighted and singled out and spread to envelop the person completely in flames. This cycle of torment continued. Though dead, yet they were alive and felt every single torment inflicted to them. I heard them repeatedly say that the devil deceived them.

Jesus said to me that many of those lost souls were prostitutes on earth. Some of them, while alive, had chosen prostitution as a means to earn their livelihood, while some had engaged in it to fund their addictions such as drugs. I saw a prostitute with a stab wound in her chest that had killed her being tormented there among many others.

Prostitutes, if you are reading this book, let me tell you that this is no means of livelihood and you will end up in hell for this sin. Please repent and save yourselves from going to that horrible place of torment.

The means by which these demons inflicted the torment was first by spears. These were no ordinary spears for they radiated fire and soon enveloped the victim in its flames. The torment did not stop there, but these souls continued to be inflicted in the particular area of sin, with sharp pins in the case of men and for women giant snakes with spikes penetrated them. I saw the lost souls of men and women cry out in terrible pain when inflicted by them. Those pathetic cries of the lost souls were endless, as were their torments.

I saw many young men and women tormented there and many more added to this never-ending human chain. Many of these lost souls were tormented by demons that changed into men while inflicting gruesome torments to men, or women while tormenting women. With sadness Jesus explained that these were homosexuals while alive and died in this sin.

I saw the lost soul of a man, a sexual pervert, being tormented by a demon that kept changing into a girl and then a boy. I could not understand why this was so. Jesus explained to me that this man had committed incest with his daughter and sodomized his son; hence the transformation of the demon to a boy and girl reflected the man's sins. The demon's transformation occurred while inflicting the horrible continual torment to the man with the spear first and then followed by sharp pins, as this lost soul cried out in agonizing pain. This cry was continual, just as the cycle of torment.

I saw another lost soul of a man being tormented by a demon that repeatedly took the form of seductive women and kept saying, "More; more," as he carried out those torments. Again I wondered why this was so. Jesus explained to me that this soul, when alive, was a pimp; and hence what the demon enacted was a reflection of the sins of this pimp.

I saw yet another soul of a man tormented by a demon that took the form of a horse while inflicting terrible torment to the lost soul. Jesus explained to me that this lost soul was a sexual pervert who had committed this sin with a horse. Hence, the horse represented the man's sin.

Reader, do you fall in this category? Are you involved in this kind of sin? Please repent of this sin and ask Jesus to cleanse you. If you do not, you will end up in hell and demons will torture you in whatever form you had indulged in sin on earth.

Sexual sin is a sin against one's own body and will take you to hell. "He who commits sexual immorality sins against his own body" (1 Cor. 6:18).

> Do you not know that the unrighteous will not inherit the kingdom of God? Do not be deceived. Neither fornicators,…nor adulterers, nor homosexuals, nor sodomites…will inherit the kingdom of God.
> —1 Corinthians 6:9–10

Before facing the judgment seat of God, be cleansed with the blood of Jesus Christ now and renounce your sin. Jesus said to the adulteress caught in sin, "Neither do I condemn you, go and sin no more" (John 8:11). And be delivered from this sinful addiction in Jesus' name: "Therefore if the Son makes you free, you shall be free indeed" (John 8:36).

Are you leading a double life today—holy on the outside yet

sexually immoral on the inside? I saw many such souls in hell. Repent today if you are involved in adultery, bestiality, fornication, homosexuality, one-night stands, pornography, incest, prostitution, or sexual perversion of any kind. Maybe the immorality you are involved in is not mentioned here; nevertheless, please repent.

Christian husbands, be faithful to your wives and love them as Christ loved the church; Christian wives, stay faithful to your husbands (Eph. 5:22–33). Be holy as God is holy. Do not cheat on each other, and let your marriage reflect the unity of Christ with the church.

Christian youths, be holy: "Let no one despise your youth, but be an example to the believers in word, in conduct, in love, in spirit, in faith, in purity" (1 Tim. 4:12).

Do not toy with sin. Toying with sin is equivalent to toying with your souls and will land you in hell. You will not find it fun then when demons inflict you with cruel tortures. Please repent and be saved.

CELEBRITY

One early morning in 2009, Jesus came to me and said, "Daughter, come with Me." Saying so, He took my hand and I instantly found us in the bedroom of a well-known celebrity who was about to die.

We stood near her bed and watched her breathe her last. After she died she found herself standing in her spirit body next to where her body lay. I could see that she was intrigued to see her spirit body, which she was seeing for the first time; but then she noticed the darkness that surrounded her and the dark path that lay ahead of her.

With that, she knew she was doomed and became intensely fearful. Heartbroken, she began to cry. She had hoped to go to heaven, and said repeatedly, "I thought I would watch over my children."

Suddenly, at this point, Jesus became visible to her. She had the following conversation with Jesus.

Celebrity: I followed the traditions of the church, so why not heaven for me?

Jesus: You did not have Me in your life. Traditions do not save you from hell; My blood does.

Celebrity: But I helped the poor. I donated to charities. I helped the poor.

Jesus: What did you do for Me?

She began to sob uncontrollably. Suddenly a huge screen from nowhere appeared in front of us. I watched her life's complete episodes played on that screen—right from the time she was born till her death. I marveled to see that each and every minute detail of her life was covered. I saw her drinking, partying—whatever she called and thought was fun. Her joys, happiness, and achievements that made her feel important, elated, and proud; every sin that she committed, every thought of sin that she had thought was only known to her; profanities she had uttered or even thought within her self were played back to her. She now realized that even her hidden thoughts of sin were actually actions that resulted in her condemnation.

After her life review ended, Jesus said sadly, "All that you had in your life was you. You worshipped yourself."

And then Jesus looked at me and said, "Every single thought a man or a woman thinks within himself or herself is an action in My sight. This is why My Word says, 'But I say to you that whoever looks at a woman to lust for her has already committed adultery with her in his heart' (Matt. 5:28)."

Beloved, our thoughts are actions in the sight of God. His Word says that He understands our thoughts afar off (Ps. 139:2). One day we will give accountability to God of what we did with our lives; that will also include our secret thought life—what we think is known only to us. Therefore, it is important to bring every thought of sin into captivity to the obedience of Christ.

Casting down arguments and every high thing that exalts itself against the knowledge of God, bringing every thought into captivity to the obedience of Christ.

—2 CORINTHIANS 10:5

And we need to be cleansed of our impurities in the blood of Jesus Christ.

As Jesus spoke to me, it appeared that He was not visible to her any longer. I saw two demons approach her as she stood condemned. They began to drag her to hell. She put up a fight and tried to resist them with all her might. But they were much too powerful for her. Jesus and I watched as she was brought to a place in hell.

At that moment she suddenly saw me. She pleaded earnestly, "Warn my family about this place, I do not want them to come here."

Those demons, the ones who had escorted her to hell, laughed at her, bowed their heads down to her, and said, "Worship you." Those two demons seemed to be especially assigned to her.

As I watched, I saw an object that suddenly appeared on her head that seemed to pierce her head. She began to scream in terrible pain. This object seemed to function similar to a suction instrument. Unable to bear the torment, she fell down on the ground. The object seemed to be embedded in her head and did not budge no matter how hard she tried to take it off her head.

And suddenly, as I watched, it was gone and had taken a sizeable portion of her head with it. As I gawked in horror, I could see that she knew and felt all that had happened to her and she screamed in agony as she lay there on the ground.

Suddenly, much to my shock, what seemed like a heavy equipment vehicle appeared there that emitted no sound at all. It was unlike anything I have seen on earth. I could see that it was used in hell to make space to accommodate more souls.

Therefore Sheol has enlarged itself And opened its mouth beyond measure; Their glory and their multitude and their pomp, And he who is jubilant, shall descend into it.

—Isaiah 5:14

Now I understood the scripture that tells us hell is never full (Prov. 27:20) in a much deeper way.

This heavy equipment vehicle buried the celebrity in deep gooey green mire as she lay there in agony. The two demons assigned to her then brought her out of there and tied her to a dead branch.

She was covered in a dirty green mud and tied to the dead branch. Suddenly I saw a fire light up from nowhere and burning with rage and she was engulfed completely in its flames.

Now, as I watched, I could see all that remained of her was a blackened burned skeleton form. As I looked closely, I saw worms crawl in and out of her skeleton form. I saw her try to brush those worms away but more seemed to come out. I marveled to see that these worms not only survived the heat of the fire but also seemed to thrive in the heat. I was reminded of the scripture mentioned in regard to hell in Mark 9:48: "Their worms do not die And fire is not quenched."

The fire never died down but continued to burn with much rage. I heard her lament, "I was young. I was pretty." I was saddened with grief to see such an end of a young life. Her torment was unending.

I kept wondering within myself regarding the dead branch since I had never seen this before in hell. I had seen other things but never this. Jesus, knowing my thoughts, answered me as He had spoken so long ago recorded in John 15:6: "If anyone does not abide in Me, he is cast out as a branch and is withered; and they gather them and throw them into the fire, and they are burned."

That explained everything to me. The dead branch was symbolic of her life on earth away from God. The Bible is true to fact; here was a literal description of what I witnessed first hand.

Jesus turned to me and said, "Death can come at any stage.

Donating to charities and keeping traditions of the church saves no one. Good works are not a substitute for salvation. Being washed in My blood and living a righteous life in My sight save a man or a woman from hell. You see, My daughter, it is all about living for Me that decides where a person will spend his or her eternity."

Reader, you might call yourself a Christian yet be living a life away from God all for yourself, as the celebrity mentioned here. Do not be deceived that you will still make it to heaven just because you followed the traditions of the church. You might have been baptized or christened as a child, but that will not take you to heaven. You need to be born again and live a life approved of God to go to heaven. Your future either in heaven or hell is based on your decision for Jesus Christ here on earth.

Please, get right with God today.

MODEL

Suddenly I was translated in my spirit and I found myself in a part of hell next to Jesus. Right in front of me, I beheld a lost soul of a woman. She was nude and had deep stab wounds all over her body. I was aghast to see such a sight. She appeared to see me and tried to cover her nakedness with her hands, for she was ashamed of her nakedness. She, however, did not seem to see Jesus.

She began to share her story. "I was a young, beautiful model; very successful in my career. One night when I returned home from work, I was knifed to death. My murderer hacked my entire body into tiny bits." With dirty grey smoke that enveloped her as she spoke, she continued, "I thought I was a Christian; I attended a church." At that moment, she saw Jesus and said, "I do not deserve to be here."

Jesus answered, "Your life was a life of sin. You committed fornication with many lovers. One enraged lover out of jealousy killed you."

She asked Jesus, "Why did my church pastor not tell me what I was doing was sin?"

Jesus answered, "You had My Word."

She went on, "Why did my mother not warn me? My mother is a Christian."

Jesus answered, "Why did you not read My Word though you kept it next to your bed?"

Sadly, we moved on. Jesus began to speak, "A lot of people call themselves Christians yet live their lives in sin. I am a Holy God. I hate sin. I would have forgiven her sins if she asked Me to. If she had renounced her evil ways, she would not have been here today."

Do not be deceived…fornicators…will [not] inherit the kingdom of God.

—1 Corinthians 6:9–10

Beloved, please do not play around with sin, for it will kill you in the end. You might consider yourself saved yet be living a life of sin. If you are in this state, you are fooling yourself that you will make it to heaven anyway. The Word of God stands forever: "The soul who sins shall die" (Ezek. 18:20).

Church pastors, please address sin as sin; without this there cannot be conviction and, hence, no repentance. Mothers and fathers, correct your children in love; you cannot turn a blind eye to their sins and let them walk into hell.

Jihadists

I was instantly translated in my spirit to a part of hell and found myself beside Jesus. We were standing amidst dense air and smoke. I recognized this as the entrance of hell.

I could see a large presence of demons frolicking about this place. Two of them passed by us speaking in an excited tone. It appeared that they had gathered here to receive someone of importance.

At this moment Jesus asked me to watch carefully. With that, I heard a deafening sound almost like a powerful explosion. I was glad to be beside Jesus for His very presence calmed and allayed my fears in this blackness of hell.

With that explosion, I could see two lost souls of men enter hell at the same time. Their entrance caused such jubilation among demons that shouted in unison, "Welcome to your paradise!" The demons then began to change simultaneously into seductive women, making lewd gestures at the lost souls, and also attempted to engage them in obscene acts saying, "We are your reward."

In vain the condemned souls tried to protest and escape. They appeared hugely disappointed and hopelessly lost. With the barrage of demons around them, it was impossible to escape from hell; rather unthinkable, as they found out soon.

As I looked at them, I wondered who were these souls and why did their presence cause such an excitement among demons. Jesus knew my thoughts and began to explain about these souls who had just lost their lives and entered hell.

Jesus said, "Daughter, these two souls were jihadists who were killed. They were important to Satan and used by him to cause extensive damage and destruction to mankind. Fully committed to their religious ideologies, they also fought for them. They planned and organized mass murders with violence. The enemy deceived them into believing that it was all for a good cause, and hence they were convinced that they were doing the right thing. They also hoped to earn their reward for laying down their lives as martyrs for this cause. Therefore, in death they had expected to be received into paradise and given the rewards as per their beliefs, including them as a part of their reward." As Jesus spoke the last part, He looked at those demons who transformed themselves into seductresses.

That explained the jihadists' disappointment that came from being let down by their false beliefs and the sheer horror of realizing that what they had lived and died for was a lie and far from the truth. I also understood now why those demons had greeted their entrance of eternal punishment as "paradise" and referred to themselves as rewards while appearing as temptresses, which added to the misery of their torment.

I could see that the welcoming mob of demons quickly changed back to their original vicious selves as they bit the lost souls with their sharp teeth and also dug their long, razorlike sharp nails into their forms. Their painful cries of horror filled the place, but still those demons did not leave these souls and engaged them in abusive, horrendous acts of perversion.

While alive, these souls had opened themselves to be used of Satan by working for him; and now, much against their will, they were controlled by demons and forced to participate in the abuse of selves.

Those demons seemed to be having a field day and exploited every possibility to abuse these two souls at all costs. The heartrending regretful cries of the lost souls realizing they wasted their entire lives for a false ideology that resulted in their eternal condemnation filled the heavy air. I could see now their mangled forms with bite marks all over them as they writhed in terrible pain.

Beloved, if you open yourself to the devil, he will abuse and ruin you. This is why the Bible warns us against giving any place to the devil (Eph. 4:27).

Their pathetic states moved me to tears. Though they had been jihadists while alive, I wondered when their ordeal would end, for this torture seemed to be never-ending. These souls were now remorseful for the terrible blunders they had made, and they also realized that they were deceived by none other than Satan himself. They repeatedly cursed themselves for this state that they were in as demons kicked their mangled forms.

Suddenly I saw a large demon approach them with two heavy chains. The same demon bound both of them with these chains and commanded this mob of demons to take them to their destination. With no ounce of strength remaining within them, they submitted to their fate at the hands of their perpetrators.

Now this mob of demons began to drag the two lost souls along a rough pathway, adding to their agony. Jesus and I followed them in much grief. It appeared much like partaking in a funeral procession, the only difference being that these were alive though dead. As these demons dragged them, they kept reminding the lost souls of their actual reward that was ahead, rubbing salt into their wounds. I could see that these lost souls were absolutely terrified of the dreadful journey ahead, yet could do nothing except lament about it. In between they also cursed themselves for their fate. Amidst this cycle of wailing, one lost soul spoke to another, "How could we be so foolish to die for this deception? What these Christians have been saying about Isa [Jesus Christ] is the truth."

The very mention of the name Isa (Jesus) enraged this mob of demons. The one who had spoken those words was kicked and asked to shut up. He was threatened with dire consequences if he dared to use that name again. The demons uttered in disgust and hatred, "We hate Him." I witnessed how uncomfortable demons get with the name of Jesus. The very name of Jesus hampers their progress and stops them in their tracks.

This journey seemed to be ongoing for a long time, and the condemned knew something terrible lay in wait ahead of them. Also, these demons laughed among themselves and jeered at them and said "special reward," though they would not say what it was. The term *special reward* made the two souls cringe in utter despair and fear, though they could not figure out within themselves what could be worse than what they had already undergone at the hands of these tormentors. In view of the dread that awaited them, they then began to beat their chests as a sign of lamentation and cried pathetically, "Doomed! Doomed!"

Immense sorrow filled my heavy heart to see their pitiful states, despite what they had done on earth. I wished to help them but knew it was impossible. I looked at Jesus; His eyes were moist with tears. Suddenly this crowd of demons shouted in glee, "We are there! We are there!" and broke into jubilant celebration. That was an indication that the lost had reached their final doom of eternal torment. The pathway led right up to a barren dead hill. These specially assigned demons now began to pull the two with renewed enthusiasm right to the top of the hill.

I wondered what lay ahead of this high hill that caused so much excitement among these demons. I sensed that there was something awful ahead. Once on top of this barren hill, I looked down. I could see a large lake that seemed to stretch real far, but I could not see how far because of the darkness that covered it. Looking at it, I could make out that this was a deep lake.

After having come face-to-face with the doom that awaited them, the condemned began to plead with these demons to spare them. As I looked at them sorrowfully, suddenly there was a loud sound. As Jesus held my hand, He said, "Look below."

I looked in awe as the lake with a great sound began to move with a violent rage and massive hot flames of fire arose out of this lake. This lake now represented a giant furnace.

Just then those demons kicked one of the lost souls into that lake. As he fell with bloodcurdling screams, instantly, as if unwrapping its anger, the fire lapped him up in its raging flames and seemed to devour the victim in its great furnace.

I waited to see in dread as to what remained of the lost soul. After a while, the flames of fire seemed to pull back and subside. Now I could see the lost soul as I looked closely. It looked as if blood was imbedded in his black burned skeleton form and he continued to burn in that state. He resembled a red-black burned skeleton form. The heavy black chain that bound him still remained intact. The fire had not devoured the heavy chain and it seemed to pull him deeper under its weight.

My heart cried as I pitied this lost soul doomed eternally in this fiery lake. Along with this lost soul, I saw many others in that lake. It was an awful sight to behold and to know that they will never be able to get out of that horrible eternal torment. Then as I watched, I saw the demons turn their attention to the other lost soul.

"Now it is your turn," those demons said to the other pitiful lost soul. After having witnessed what was in store for him, this lost soul cried louder and louder. Suddenly he saw me, and I froze in fear at the thought that I was visible to those demons. Jesus held my hand and said, "Daughter, none of the demons can hear or see you." That statement calmed and rid me of my fears.

At this point, this jihadist began to speak to me, "Warn jihadists like us not to come here. Tell them not to waste their lives for a false ideology. There is no paradise for us. No rewards. It is only a deception to bring us here." As he said those words, he was kicked by those demons into this lake of fire. I was saddened beyond words to hear the helpless, dreadful cries that filled the place.

As he fell into this lake, the flames of fire, which appeared to have subsided, came back with much rage, took him in, and rose to a great height. The devouring flames within this lake seemed to have sprung in action with the arrival of a victim with its jaws of death just as a lion to its prey. After a while the fire seemed to subside again. Then as I saw him, he looked similar to the other lost soul—a red-black skeleton with his chain remaining. He was dead yet living in eternal torment, like all others in this place. I could not see the other lost soul in this lake.

I was grieved in my spirit to see such a sight. I could see that Jesus was sorrowful. He began to speak to me, "I came for the sinners to come to repentance (Luke 5:32) and 'I have no pleasure in the death of the wicked, but that the wicked turn from his way and live' (Ezek. 33:11). Warn the wicked not to come here."

With that, I found myself back on earth. As I write this, their agonizing cries still ring in my ears. If you are a jihadist, please repent of your deeds. You are not reading this by chance. Jesus wants to save you from hell. Unless you repent and seek His forgiveness, your end will be as those jihadists mentioned above. They found out too late that they were wrong. Please do not be like them. There is no paradise for murderers. There is only one way to go to heaven and that is through Jesus Christ.

The Bible calls Satan a murderer and a liar:

He was a murderer from the beginning, and does not stand in the truth, because there is no truth in him. When he speaks a lie, he speaks from his own resources, for he is a liar and the father of it.

—JOHN 8:44

To murder is a sin, and murderers end up in the lake of fire: "But...murderers shall have their part in the lake which burns with fire and brimstone, which is the second death" (Rev. 21:8).

Please repent of this heinous crime. Committing murder is not and will never be a good cause. You are being deceived by Satan and are working for him. He hates mankind created by God and seeks to kill them by inciting them against one another. Please repent now and give up your false beliefs.

Only Jesus can forgive your sins: "If we confess our sins, He is faithful and just to forgive us our sins and to cleanse us from all unrighteousness" (1 John 1:9).

Finally, heaven is not a place for carnal gratification. To live for carnal fulfillment is sin and not from God, as the Bible mentions. Living according to this sinful nature results in eternal death. The lust of the eyes, the lust of the flesh, and the pride of life are not from God (1 John 2:16); and if you live according to the sinful nature you will die (Rom. 8:13). God is holy and without practicing holiness, no one can see God (Heb. 12:14).

In other words, you cannot even think of entering heaven if you live in sin. Seeking forgiveness of sins in Jesus Christ and living a life of obedience based on the Bible, the Word of God, qualifies you for heaven.

I sincerely pray that you do not reject the message of Jesus Christ; if you do you will end up in hell. You will regret and repent then, but it will be too late. Do not miss this opportunity to come to Jesus.

TERRORIST

Jesus appeared to me and said, "Daughter, come with Me." Instantly I was away in my spirit with Him to a part of hell. I found myself standing next to Jesus atop a dry dead hill. At that instant I saw a powerful demon approach the hill with a lost soul. As they came nearer, I could see that this demon had a single horn on his head, a single eye in the center of his forehead, hooves for feet, and crocodile-like sharp and powerful claws for hands; his very look evoked terror.

I recognized this lost soul as one of the most wanted terrorists in the world. I was shocked to see this well-known terrorist here, since I was not aware of his death, as there had been no mention of him in the media. Therefore, in my curiosity, I asked Jesus "Lord, when did he die?" Jesus answered, "Just now." This terrorist had attracted worldwide attention for his ruthless acts of terrorism. In much contrast to his portrayed image of a hardcore militant, he now appeared completely terrified and powerless in front of this brutish giant demon.

I could see that this lost soul was bound by a thick, black rope and that the demon grasped the rear end of this rope firmly in between his claws. At that moment Jesus corrected me and said that it was a chain and not a rope. This chain appeared similar to a rope, and I mistook it for one since I had never seen a chain like that on earth before.

Jesus told me that this terrorist was confident right to the end that he would not be caught, but he was found and shot dead. Instead of being remorseful for his wicked deeds, he appeared to be angry with himself for having been caught and shot dead. All that he kept saying to himself was, "I never thought I will be caught," and then he punched himself in anger.

I was horrified to see dried blood embedded all over his form. Jesus said, "This soul took countless lives mercilessly; hence, the blood of all those lives is upon him and will never go away."

Neither the lost soul nor the one-eyed demon appeared to see us. The demon stood him atop the hill and pointed below. I could see the lake of fire there. The demon said to the condemned soul, "This is your condemnation." At that very moment with a great sound, the lake moved. The flames of fire within the lake seemed to be stirred into action by the presence of a readied victim about to enter its furnace of affliction. I watched as the demon kicked this soul into the fiery lake. Screams of horror filled the place as the condemned soul of the terrorist spiraled down the vortex of his doom.

His voice died down amidst the devouring giant flames of fire in the lake. After a while, as those flames appeared to pull back their merciless rage and smoldered down, I spotted this lost soul as I looked closely. He now appeared a red-black, burned skeleton yet his black chain remained and the blood of the countless lives remained embedded on his burned form. The fire had not consumed them and spared them as marks of his unrighteousness.

Jesus said to me, "Daughter, warn the terrorists of what awaits them if they do not repent." With that I found myself back on earth and shared about this particular terrorist's damnation in hell with my husband. But he did not believe me since there was no mention about this terrorist's death in the media. The very next day the media blasted the report of this world-famed militant's death giving wide coverage in detail regarding the manner in which he was caught and shot dead. The media confirmed his death and the day on which he was killed. Beloved, that was the exact day I saw this terrorist in hell, condemned and tormented in the lake of fire. My husband apologized for his unbelief.

Reader, if you were to die now, you will find yourself on your way either to heaven or hell, just as it says in the Bible.

If you are a terrorist, please repent now; for if you die in this state, you will end up in the lake of fire where you will be tormented forever, like the famed terrorist mentioned above. God loves you and has a provision for you to be saved in Jesus Christ. He alone can forgive your sins. You are not reading this by chance. This is an opportunity given to you by God to save you from hell. Please repent and be saved in Jesus' name.

Do not be confident that you will never be caught like the terrorist mentioned above. You are being deceived by Satan that what you are doing is the right thing. To murder and destroy the lives of others is a sin; moreover, their blood is upon you. Only the blood of Jesus can cleanse that stain of murder that is upon you. You can never get away with your wickedness. Your sins will find you out, as the Bible says, "You have sinned against the LORD; and be sure your sin will find you out" (Num. 32:23).

I have witnessed the horror that awaits you if you do not repent; and I appeal to you, please do not go there. Give up those activities, turn to Jesus, and He will save you. Do not shut Him out, for He is the *only* way to stay away from hell. I sincerely hope that you will not reject His love.

ATHEIST

In 2012 suddenly Jesus appeared. He came near and held my hand. With that I found us in a part of hell. I could hear vehement cries of a man that seemed to be coming from directly ahead of us. As we walked along a long stretch of a burned and dry path that led to a mound, the desperate cries grew louder and louder.

We stepped onto the mound where the path ended. I could see below a blackened skeleton form of a man submerged in lake of fire and his black burned face alone jutted out. Now his cries turned to moans. He never looked up even once, which gave me the picture that he was not aware of our presence. He kept lamenting constantly, "I did not believe in God. I did not believe in God…"

Jesus began to speak to me, "While alive, this man was a scientist. He prided in his intellect and found it difficult to believe My existence. He rejected My existence and dismissed My Word as the babbling of fools. He won many awards and was known universally for his achievements. The world called him a great scientist. After his death, he realized he had made a huge mistake and that he had been deceived by the enemy. He has been here for a long time."

Contrary to my belief that this soul could not see us because he never once looked up, Jesus said to me, "Daughter, he can see us. Once proud of his achievements and the accolades of men he received as a result of his achievements while alive, now he is ashamed of those very things in which he once took pride. He regrets that he failed to know Me while considering himself wise. That is the reason he does not look up at Me. What he constantly laments is his acknowledgement of sin." As soon as Jesus said those words, this lost soul, still not looking up, began to sob and said, "I am unworthy to face the Creator whose existence I denied. Warn the scientists not to come here."

As this lost soul spoke, the fire from within the lake swept over him with a rushing sound and submerged him completely in its flames and his voice died down. I could not hear or see him anymore.

Jesus said sadly, "There are many like him here," and pointed toward the lake. I could see several other blackened skeleton forms in this boundless lake of fire that spanned across the place.

You might be a scientist today and pride yourself in your intellect; but please listen to me. There is a great God who created this universe; and one day, after death, you will face Him. No matter what achievements and awards you have won in this world, after your death those awards will hold no meaning. You will be lost for eternity and will be like any other lost soul there in hell. So please do not reject Jesus Christ. He alone gives you life. Humble yourself as a child and receive Him in your heart.

> Assuredly, I say to you, unless you are converted and become as little children, you will by no means enter the kingdom of heaven.
>
> —MATTHEW 18:3

Please, do not be like this scientist who was wise in his own eyes and ended up in hell, much to his disbelief and shame.

> Let no one deceive himself. If anyone among you seems to be wise in this age, let him become a fool that he may become wise. For the wisdom of this world is foolishness with God. For it is written, "He catches the wise in their own craftiness."
>
> —1 CORINTHIANS 3:18–19

FAMOUS SINGERS

Jesus held my hand, and instantly I found us standing next to an open fiery pit. I could see two burned blackened hands stretch out of that pit. On a close inspection, I could see that this was the lost soul of a woman. She appeared to be in liquid fire and in continual torment.

Suddenly her form changed and I identified her as a famous celebrity singer while alive. Amidst her groans, as she tried to brush away worms that crawled out of her, she suddenly saw Jesus and said, "Please get me out of here. I was foolish, so foolish, when alive. The fatal accidental mix of drugs and liquor killed me. I cannot believe I did that to myself. I had a fantastic career in front of me. I was famous. I had many fans—so many of them—and they worshipped me. They made me feel like a goddess. Get me out of here. Send me back to the world and I will tell people; I will tell my fans; I will tell all of them about You. I will not smoke, do drugs, or consume liquor anymore. I do not want them anymore. Please get me out of here. Please, please."

The desperate pleas of this once famous celebrity singer, who died accidentally after the fatal mix, aggrieved me beyond words. Jesus explained to me that, while alive, she was a slave of cigarettes, drugs, and liquor. Now in torment, she hated those very things she had loved on earth.

Jesus began to speak to this lost soul, "You get to live only once, after which is the judgment. You are accountable for the talent I gave you to be used for My glory. 'He who is not with Me, is against Me' (Matt. 12:30). Your worship was directed to your own self. I gave you many chances to repent. There were times before when you tried the same thing, yet you did not die. Those were the chances I gave you to repent. Now it is too late. I will save as long as one is alive; but after death, judgment is set."

Saying this, Jesus moved away from that pit and said to me, "Daughter, I will show you several more of these once famous people on earth who were idol worshipped."

Beloved, you might be a well-known artist today. Let me warn you; do not try to experiment with your life like this mentioned one-time famous artist. Please repent and use your talent for the glory of God. He will hold you accountable for the talent He has blessed you with. After death, you will hate the very things you were enslaved to on earth, just like this artist.

As soon as Jesus spoke those words, I instantly found us in front of a cell. I could see a lost soul of another well-known singer inside this cell. His form changed from the famous figure he was when alive to a burned skeleton form. He kept miming as if to sing while he continued to dance non-stop.

Jesus told me, "This is what he loved to do on earth while alive. One must reap what one has sown."

I saw two demons inside his cell and they laughed and jeered at him saying, "Hail...," as they bowed their heads in front of him as he cursed them with profanities.

I heard him say, "All I want is to sleep and rest." As soon as he uttered those words, both the demons kicked him and commanded him to sing. They also began to torment him in such a profligate manner that I cannot describe. He cried for mercy and pleaded them to stop the torment, to which they replied, "This was your life. You enjoyed these on earth."

He appeared to see neither Jesus nor me. He was lost in his own torment and blamed himself for his death and to have landed in hell. I heard him lament, "Why did I not accept the gospel that was presented to me? There is no peace, no rest here."

With that, we moved away from that cell and Jesus stopped in front of yet another cell.

I could see inside that cell was the lost soul of another famous personality. This once world-renowned singer had even sung in praises of Jesus. As I watched this lost soul, who was in much torment in flames of fire, suddenly he saw me and said, "I thought that Jesus is *one* of the many ways to God. I did not realize till my death that He is the *only* way. How I wish I had believed that while alive. I even sung His praises; and now those songs are a constant reminder of the opportunities I had on earth to receive Him as the only way to God." He wept bitterly as he said those words. I noticed that his tears would appear and then disappear as fast as they came.

Sadly we moved on to another cell. Jesus stopped in front of a cell. I could see a lost soul of yet another celebrity singer inside that cell.

She wept uncontrollably. She appeared to see me and said, "I was done away with. I wish I had known what was ahead of me. I know now that talking about Jesus and living for Him are completely two different things."

Suddenly she saw Jesus and began to plead, "Please get me out of here. I sang for You. Get me out."

Jesus looked at her sorrowfully and said, "Woman, singing for Me does not save you from hell. You never sought to leave your addictions, and as a result you died. If only you had asked Me, I would have forgiven your sins and broken the power of sin over your life. I gave you many opportunities to repent. Now it is too late; too late."

With that, she began to wail, saying, "The pleasures of the world killed me. Why did I not listen to my mother?" She now regretted not giving up her sinful addictions.

My dear reader, you might be an award-winning artist and possibly even sing in praise of Jesus like the mentioned celebrity singers.

No matter how many awards you have won or how famous you are in this world, if you do not have Jesus in your life as your Savior and renounce your sin, you are doomed and on your way to hell. Once you die, you will regret your worldly achievements and recognition that you were proud of on earth while alive. The famous personalities I met in hell were winners of many awards, renowned globally, and idol worshipped by millions of fans; yet they all regret the very things that they were known for and proud about while alive.

> For what will it profit a man if he gains the whole world, and loses his own soul?
>
> —MARK 8:36

Your talent is given of God for His glory, and you are accountable as to what you do with your talent. Are there any addictions in your life? Remember, if you come to Jesus and repent, He will not only forgive your sins but also set you free from sinful addictions in your life.

Jesus also told me that many famous celebrities languishing in hell had sold their souls to Satan in exchange for fame, recognition, riches, and power. And all of them had died unexpectedly and ended up in hell. Jesus told me that He blessed them as they started to sing praises for Him; but when fame and riches came knocking at their doors, they turned away from Him and made pacts with Satan in greed for much more.

We continued to walk past several of these cells. Suddenly Jesus stopped in front of yet another cell. I could see that inside this cell was a lost soul of yet another celebrity singer who was very well known in his time.

He appeared to be tormented by a giant snake that seemed to suffocate him. In doing so, it appeared as if flames of fire came out of this snake. I watched in bewilderment the unending torment this lost soul was subjected to. Just then, Jesus began to speak, making things plain for me, "While alive, this lost soul made a pact with Satan for worldly achievements and power. This snake that you see is a demon in the form of a snake. This demon inhabited him while alive, and even spoke through him. At his death the same snake, the one he let live inside of him and speak through him, is tormenting him."

I watched as this lost soul begged this snake to just let him die. With that, the serpent hissed at him and said in a guttural voice, "This is your death," and laughed.

Budding singers, accomplished and well-known artists, please do not make pacts with Satan for worldly achievements. Satan is not your friend and hates you. He does not give anything for free; he does it only to get your souls to hell for eternal torment.

Fame, riches, and power are worthless once you die. You will regret it all once you go to that place of torment.

Your soul is precious, so very precious that the devil wants it really bad; he wants to take you to that place that was prepared for him and his demons. Please do not exchange your souls for temporary worldly pleasures. And if you did happen to make a pact with Satan, you can still break it in Jesus' name while you are alive. Repent and renounce your sin, and Jesus will forgive you. Remember, there is hope while you are alive; after death it is too late.

FAMOUS ACTORS

Jesus said, "Daughter, there is more to see." I was instantly translated to a different part of hell where once famous actors, actresses, and movie directors of the famed Hollywood and around the world were languishing.

I beheld a lost soul of a legendary Hollywood actress inside a cell. She seemed to see me and began to speak, introducing herself: "I was very beautiful and enjoyed every bit of attention I received because of it. I had many lovers. However, I wanted to marry one of them but he would not marry me. Soon after, I was killed and landed here." She continued, "One day, as I was traveling in my car, a pastor went past on his cycle. He recognized me and said, 'Whatever you have in this world, you will lose; but what Jesus gives, you will never lose.' I looked down on him for he was shabbily dressed. I realized the truth in his statement after my death and coming to hell."

She was a burned skeleton form with no eyes; but to my amazement, twice tears came in those empty sockets where once eyes were and they dried as fast as they came as she said those words. She pleaded with me remorsefully, "Please warn the young women not to imitate me and my sinful lifestyle. I am paying for my sins. I have been here so long." As she said those words, I saw sparks of fire light up her cell. She lamented, "If only I had listened to that pastor, I would not be here today."

I was immensely sorrowful and wanted badly to help her, but I knew it was impossible. Unlike others I had witnessed, she made no attempts, no pleadings for the torment to stop; but instead she said, "I am paying for my sins."

In sorrow we walked away from her cell to yet another cell. I could see a lost soul of a once famous actress. She had died very young; while alive she was much loved for her beauty.

I cringed in horror as her form changed to a blackened burned skeleton form, much in contrast to her once beautiful self. She did not appear to notice us, as she was lost in her unending torment, which was too great.

We walked away from her cell in sorrow. Going past the cells, we came to the place where the pits were. Jesus stopped in front of one such pit. I could see a lost soul of a legendary actor burn in flames of fire in an open pit.

He saw me and said, "I went on a pilgrimage and visited all the sacred places. No pastor ever told me about Jesus—that He is the *only* one who saves." With that, he began to curse the pastors.

Jesus said to me, "This lost soul, while alive, had heard about Me—though not through the pastors—yet he refused to accept Me.

After his death he blames the pastors for this state of torment that he is in."

Beloved, do not wait to accept the good news of salvation. It doesn't matter whether the messenger of the good news is a pastor or not.

Pastors, please do not shy away from sharing the gospel in front of well-known and influential people of the world.

We moved away from that pit. After crossing several other pits, Jesus came and stood in front of a particular pit. Amidst the flames of fire, I saw the lost soul of a legendary actor who was also a movie director while alive.

His form changed from the famous figure he once was to a burned skeleton form. He had not been prepared for his death that came unexpectedly. While alive, he had believed in reincarnation; but after death he was brought to hell instead. Suddenly he saw me and began to speak, "I did not know that Jesus was this important. After coming here, I understand that it is important to live for Him while alive. I wish I had believed this truth that He alone saves. I wasted my life acting and directing all those movies. I prided in my intellect and thought it was utter foolishness to believe in salvation. Now I understand what my wife had been telling about Jesus is all true. How I wish I had listened to her. Every time she came speaking about Jesus and His forgiveness, I asked her to shut up and told her that I did not have the time for that nonsense. I lived my life as I wanted to and did not believe that death would come to me. Now I have eternity to regret."

He sobbed with a loud voice as he said those words; and then he continued, "If only I had believed about Jesus I would have done everything for Him and not wasted my time acting and directing those worthless movies. I won many awards for them but all that is of no value here. I was so proud of all my achievements. I was a fool. I have wasted my life on earth."

Jesus looked at me and said sorrowfully, "His wife is a Christian, and she shared many times about Me. But he dismissed it all, and said that she was a fool to believe all that and that no intelligent man would ever believe in salvation for it does not make sense. Now he regrets his life that he wasted on earth."

Beloved, are your views similar to this movie director? The Bible says, "Let no one deceive himself. If anyone among you seems to be wise in this age, let him become a fool that he may become wise. For the wisdom of this world is foolishness with God" (1 Cor. 3:18–19).

You might be a movie director today. Do not be like this lost soul who found out too late, after his death, that without Jesus he is lost. Repent today and be saved before it's time to pack off from this world. The things of this world—including those awards you might have won, recognition, and fame—are of value as long as you are alive. After death, those very things you valued on earth will become irrelevant.

Glorify God through all your talents: "Whatever you do, do all to the glory of God" (1 Cor. 10:31).

God Men

Jesus held my hand and we moved away from that pit. We walked for a while and came to a place where there were several enclosed cells. I had not come across cells like these before in hell. I could hear deafening screams coming from the cells, and I understood that souls were trapped in these cells. Dumbfounded, I asked Jesus, "Why are the lost souls in there, dear Lord?"

He began to explain, "These lost souls, when alive, were renowned globally and idol worshipped as gods. Satan used them to dupe masses, and he gave them special powers to perform miracles. Many were deceived by them and left their families, sold their properties, gave all to follow them, and served them wholeheartedly. While alive, these god men had believed that after their death they would be reincarnated, but ended up here instead."

With that, Jesus stopped in front of one such cell. He said that each enclosed cell housed an open pit. I instantly found us inside this cell. I saw demons present in large numbers inside the enclosed cell. I could see a lost soul of a man who was famously worshipped as a god while alive. This god man was used to a life of luxury and was served readily by many devotees. Much in contrast, now he was controlled by these demons. He appeared to be a puppet in their hands and forced to obey their orders.

Jesus told me that these were the demons who had worked for him in earth—the ones he had believed he had control over. I watched in horror as those demons subjected him to intense torture. I could see them bite him all over with their sharp animal-like teeth as he cried out in sharp pain. Then they sat him on a giant coiled snake. This was in mockery of the throne he had always occupied in the presence of his many worshippers.

It appeared as if the giant serpent was disturbed from its slumber as the lost soul sat on it. The snake hissed at him in fury and coiled around him. The lost soul was no match for this giant snake. As I watched, the snake began to suffocate him. He begged to be let out of its grip as the demons laughed and the snake appeared to tighten its grip with each of his beggings.

After some time the snake started to loosen its coil around this god man and released him. Now what remained of this god man was his bloodied, disfigured form. The demons threw the god man immediately into the fiery pit prepared for him within this enclosed cell. The open fiery pit burned with raging fire. As his screams died down to sobs, I heard him say, "I was god."

With that, Jesus led me outside that cell and said to me, "Daughter, I will show you another such god man." He stopped in front of another enclosed cell. And instantly I found us inside this cell. I could see the lost soul of a famous god man who had promoted sexual perversion and had several thousands of ardent worshippers. He had believed in reincarnation after death, but much to his shock he ended up in hell.

I saw this god man subjected to grotesque acts of perversion and tormented by several demons present inside this cell. He cried for mercy but there was none and no respite from that never-ending torment. I saw those demons as they bit him all over and engaged him in such acts of wickedness. While inflicting these things, they kept reminding him how much he had enjoyed the acts on earth. As I watched, those demons dispatched him to the open fiery pit burning with rage within this cell.

I could hear him lament and wail as we walked out of there. Jesus said, "Wickedness is repaid with wickedness." "The body is not for sexual immorality but for the Lord" (1 Cor. 6:13).

This god man reaped in eternity what he had sown on earth. With death, he awoke to his condemnation. If you sow corruption, you will also reap corruption (Gal. 6:8).

The Bible says, "All flesh is as grass, And all the glory of man as the flower of the grass. The grass withers, And its flower falls away" (1 Pet. 1:24).

> Do not be deceived, God is not mocked; for whatever a man sows, that he will also reap.
> —GALATIANS 6:7

Reader, if you consider yourself a god man, please repent. The two god men I witnessed in hell had several thousand followers who worshipped them, yet that did not save them from going to hell. Believe in Jesus Christ and you will be saved.

You can be idol worshipped but that does not make you a god. You are being deceived by Satan. Sin results in death. "The wages of sin is death" (Rom. 6:23).

Acknowledge humbly that you are a sinner. Forgiveness of sins is offered *only* in Jesus Christ; and unless you sincerely repent, you will end up in hell and those demons you think you can control on earth will control and torture you in hell.

Come to Jesus without any delay and live.

Chapter Twelve

CHRISTIANS IN HELL

BACKSLIDDEN

IN 2003 I was translated in my spirit to a part of hell and found myself next to Jesus. He asked me to watch carefully. This place appeared to be an open ground, and I could see a lost soul of a man made to work very hard under the supervision of demons. They monitored his every single movement. This soul seemed to have no moment of rest and appeared to be much fearful of these demons.

This lost soul appeared to be unloading and filling what appeared like a trolley with a large amount of coal, and then transporting these in the heavy trolley to a destined place. I could see that these evil demons ordered him about and yelled at him to be quick as he continued with his work single-handedly without help, in much fear. This work seemed to be unending.

Suddenly this lost soul saw me. Though he was a blackened, burned form, I could see the absolute terror displayed on his skeletal face.

Jesus told me that this lost soul, while alive, was once a born-again Christian and had even testified in water baptism; but he had backslidden and died in that state. Demons enjoy tormenting these souls who once belonged to Jesus and make them work very hard.

In 2005 suddenly I was translated in my spirit to a part in hell and beheld a lost soul of a man. I could see that he had metal implanted on his right leg by surgery; and though he was in a blackened burned skeleton form, this was clearly visible on his form. I saw him forced to work hard by demons, and under their supervision carried out the similar task as mentioned above. There was no respite, the torment was unending. I could sense the immense fear in the lost soul.

Jesus told me that this soul also was a born-again Christian once, but had backslidden into a life of sin and died unexpectedly in that state.

Beloved, were you born again once but have backslidden now? Please repent, for if you die in this state, you will not make it to heaven. Once you are born again, do not be entangled again with sin, for it will kill you in the end. Please come back to Jesus now.

> Stand fast therefore in the liberty by which Christ has made us free, and do not be entangled again with a yoke of bondage.
>
> —GALATIANS 5:1

DECEIVED

One evening in 2008, suddenly I was instantly translated in my spirit to a part in hell. I could see groups of lost souls chained together. I could see "DECEIVED" written on each of them. I heard these lost souls say, "I was deceived." These lost souls appeared to be hopelessly lost and in tremendous pain.

Jesus explained to me that these souls knew about Him, yet were slaves of sin and died in the bondage of their sins. These souls were deceived into believing that they would still make it to heaven. I saw these lost souls as chained. The chain represented the bondage of their sin. "His own iniquities entrap the wicked man, And he is caught in the cords of his sin" (Prov. 5:22).

As we stood in front of a group of chained souls, suddenly a young man cried out, "Jesus! Jesus!" I understood then that Jesus was visible to him. This lost soul was crying out to Jesus, "I served You! Get me out of here!"

His heartrending cries moved me to tears. Jesus looked at him sadly and said, "You lived a life of sin. You claimed to serve Me but lived in fornication. You knew that My Word says fornicators will not enter My kingdom (1 Cor. 6:9)."

The lost soul began to sob aloud, "I thought that was a little sin and You would not mind since I served you full-time." Jesus looked at him and said, "You were deceived."

Beloved, the Word of God calls us to "walk as the children of light" (Eph. 5:8) and to "be doers of the word, and not hearers only, deceiving yourselves" (James 1:22). You can call yourself a Christian, yet live a life of sin. If we call ourselves His children, let us also walk in truth.

Just then there was a loud cry of a woman. Jesus told me that this woman was born again once but willfully married an idol worshipper. Jesus looked at this lost soul angrily and said to her, "You rejected Me and compromised by marrying an idol worshipper. I wanted you to have a godly home and raise godly seed. You have profaned My institution of marriage."

She replied," I thought You would not mind if I married an idol worshipper."

Jesus replied, "You were deceived. There is no hope now."

I saw another lost soul of a man who was chained and in much torment. Jesus said to me that this lost soul knew about Him, yet he was not willing to give up his sinful addiction and died in that state suddenly.

These souls had never desired to be freed from their bondage of sin. Jesus told me, "If only they had asked Me to forgive their sins and set them free from their sin, I would have broken that bondage of sin over their lives and they need not be in hell today."

Beloved, you might be a Christian but living in bondage to sin. Please repent, asking God to break that power of sin over your life. "So if the Son sets you free, you will be free indeed" (John 8:36, NIV).

HYPOCRITES

> Then the Lord said to him, "Now you Pharisees make the outside of the cup and dish clean, but your inward part is full of greed and wickedness."
>
> —LUKE 11:39

In 2012 I beheld lost souls of Christians in a part of hell that appeared like a dead valley. In this blackness of hell, through the light of Jesus I could see these lost souls in black robes weeping and gnashing their teeth.

Jesus explained to me regarding these lost souls, "Daughter, these were the hypocrites who appeared pious on the outside but full of wickedness in the inside. While alive, they had honored Me with their lips but their lives were in darkness far away from Me. Their black robes signify their state of darkness in sin in which they died. While alive, they loved the darkness and not the light; and this is what they have received an eternal darkness of separation away from Me after their death."

> Inasmuch as these people draw near with their mouths and honor Me with their lips, But have removed their hearts far from Me, And their fear toward Me is taught by the commandment of men.
>
> —ISAIAH 29:13

LIARS

> All liars shall have their part in the lake which burns with fire and brimstone, which is the second death.
>
> —REVELATION 21:8

In 2009 I beheld lost souls of those Christians who had lied for personal gains and died in that state. I also beheld those who had compromised with the truth of God's Word to please people. Jesus termed these people as liars. I saw them tormented in the lake of fire.

I saw one such lost soul of a man who had been baptized in the Holy Spirit but went back to his church that did not believe in the anointing of the Holy Spirit. His church found out and questioned him about it. Fearing rebuttal from the church that he was a member of, he denied the whole thing, saying he did not know what they were talking about. He also said that he did not believe the anointing of the Holy Spirit existed. He died in that state and ended up in hell.

This lost soul cried, "Warn people out there not to do what I did."

Jesus said, "There are many like him here."

Beloved, the truth of the Word of God cannot be compromised. If you know the truth and yet compromise to please people around you, you will be counted as a liar once you depart from this world.

I saw another lost soul who had lied and died in that state. This was the lost soul of a woman. This woman, while alive, was a pastor's wife and had acquired the church property as her own through fraudulent means.

Time passed and she died. Now she is burning in the flames of fire for the sin she committed. I beheld her blackened burned skeleton form. With folded skeletal hands, she pleaded me to warn the people of the world not to do what she did. She said, "It is not worth it. The torment is too great here."

The Word of God commands us to stand for the truth. Repent if you have lied and acquired things for yourself that did not belong to you. To lie is an attribute of Satan, whom the Bible says "is a liar and the father of it" (John 8:44). The Bible records the story of Ananias and Sapphira who sold their possession and kept back part of the proceeds. Ananias, with the knowledge of his wife, Sapphira, brought a certain part and laid it at Peter's feet. Filled with the Holy Spirit, Peter knew that Ananias had lied. It is clear from the scripture that Ananias and Sapphira were struck dead as a punishment. Peter termed their lying as not lying to men but to God.

But a certain man named Ananias, with Sapphira his wife, sold a possession. And he kept back part of the proceeds, his wife also being aware of it, and brought a certain part and laid it at the apostles' feet. But Peter said, "Ananias, why has Satan filled your heart to lie to the Holy Spirit and keep back part of the price of the land for yourself? While it remained, was it not your own? And after it was sold, was it not in your own control? Why have you conceived this thing in your heart? You have not lied to men but to God." Then Ananias, hearing these words, fell down and breathed his last. So great fear came upon all those who heard these things. And the young men arose and wrapped him up, carried him out, and buried him. Now it was about three hours later when his wife came in, not knowing what had happened. And Peter answered her, "Tell me whether you sold the land for so much?" She said, "Yes, for so much." Then Peter said to her, "How is it that you have agreed together to test the Spirit of the Lord? Look, the feet of those who have buried your husband are at the door, and they will carry you out." Then immediately she fell down at his feet and breathed her last. And the young men came in and found her dead, and carrying her out, buried her by her husband.

—Acts 5:1–10

Mishandlers of God's Money

One night in 2008 I was translated in my spirit to a part of hell where I saw a multitude of men and women with their hands tied behind their backs burning in flames of fire. I could not see where this line of people ended, no matter how much I tried to.

Jesus told me, "These souls, while alive, held important positions in the church and ministry and misused My money for their own purposes. With the money people had entrusted them for My work, some of these souls even bought houses and other things for personal use. These were the people who had preached My Word and knew My Word, many of whom were pastors in the churches. They had never dreamt that after their death they would end up here."

Jesus also said that many among these lost souls had come into ministry not with the passion to see the lost saved, but for the greed of money.

> Her heads judge for a bribe, Her priests teach for pay, and her prophets divine for money. Yet they lean on the LORD, and say, "Is not the LORD among us? No harm can come upon us."
>
> —MICAH 3:11

These lost souls were not aware of the presence of Jesus or me but were lost in their own torment. I could feel the intense heat of the fire as I stood there.

Preachers, teachers, people involved in ministry, please be faithful with God's money. God is faithful and He will provide for you if you are true to Him; but please do not spend that money you have been entrusted with His work for your own purposes. Please remember, you are accountable to God as to what you do with His money.

All those people I witnessed in hell had spent God's money on themselves instead of utilizing it for the purpose it was entrusted to them for; as a result they ended in hell. "You cannot serve God and mammon" (Matt. 6:24).

> For the love of money is a root of all kinds of evil, for which some have strayed from the faith in their greediness, and pierced themselves through with many sorrows.
>
> —1 TIMOTHY 6:10

Please do not convert God's ministry into a money making business enterprise. God will hold you accountable for this. You might get away with it in this world, but after death there is no escape. Please repent now.

MOCKERS OF THE WORD

> Know this first of all, that in the last days mockers will
> come with their mocking, following after their own lusts.
> —2 PETER 3:3, NAS

In 2010 I beheld a lost soul of a man who was thrown in a part of
hell where the ground was wet and swampy. I could see that there
were many others like him there. I heard this lost soul weep and
lament. He sobbed out loud, "I wish I had not mocked God's Word
and accepted it just as it is." I saw a heavy equipment vehicle there
that emitted no sound yet dug deeper in this slimy earth, pushing
the lost souls deeper and deeper inside the mire. I could see demons
watch over them. It was impossible to ever get out of there.

Jesus told me, "These lost souls that you see are the ones who had
mocked My Word while alive. They did not understand My Word
but spoke evil of it. If they had sought Me in truth, I would have
taught them My Word through My Spirit."

> But these, like natural brute beasts made to be caught and
> destroyed, speak evil of the things they do not understand,
> and will utterly perish in their own corruption.
> —2 PETER 2:12

Beloved, please do not mock the Word of God. It is to be accepted
in its totality, not for you to pick and choose what you agree with
and dismiss what you do not agree with.

> All Scripture is given by inspiration of God, and is profit-
> able for doctrine, for reproof, for correction, for instruction
> in righteousness, that the man of God may be complete,
> thoroughly equipped for every good work.
> —2 TIMOTHY 3:16–17

God has magnified His Word above His name; therefore, it is to be esteemed highly in our lives: "For You have magnified Your word above all Your name" (Ps. 138:2).

You might be a person who is unable to understand the Bible. It was written by the Spirit of God. It can only be discerned spiritually and needs to be understood in God's light and wisdom through His Holy Spirit. It will not make sense if you try to reason it out logically. Do not limit the Word of God to your limitation. By submitting in humility to God, you become a pupil under the great Teacher; so let go of your arguments, conditions, and limitations and let Him reveal Himself to you beyond your mental barriers.

Unfruitful

In 2007 I beheld the souls of the lost who were unfruitful burning in raging flames of fire. Jesus said, "They all knew about Me and what My Word said about bearing good fruit for Me. Yet they lived selfish, self-centered lives. They were neither examples as Christians nor sharers of the good news with others, believing that was their pastor's responsibility."

These lost souls saw Jesus and pleaded, "Send us back now! We will bear fruit for You." Without a word, Jesus led me away from there.

> And even now the ax is laid to the root of the trees. Therefore every tree which does not bear good fruit is cut down and thrown into the fire.
>
> —Matthew 3:10

Beloved, Jesus is the Bread of Life and needs to be shared with others so that their lives can be enriched like yours. In turn, they will enrich others. God wants you to be a channel of blessing for others. If you contain the good news only to yourself, those souls who could have been touched through you will remain deprived of the blessing God would have them receive through you. Therefore, be examples as Christians and witness, bearing much fruit for Him. Sharing the good news of salvation is each Christian's responsibility and not just a pastor's.

> For it is the God who commanded light to shine out of darkness, who has shone in our hearts to give the light of the knowledge of the glory of God in the face of Jesus Christ.
>
> —2 Corinthians 4:6

Wicked Servants

In 2012 I was instantly translated to a part of hell. I found myself standing in front of a cell beside Jesus. I could see a lost soul of a man inside this cell who was bound with a chain and beaten. This lost soul wept out loud. In horror, I asked Jesus, "Lord, what did this soul do to deserve this?" Jesus answered, "While alive, this man was a pastor and was not found faithful in My work. I blessed him as he started his ministry and began to use him. But as he became popular, he began to misuse the office of pastor, started a cult, and deceived many. He led them away from the knowledge of the truth. In that state, he died and was brought here."

> And that servant who knew his master's will, and did not prepare himself or do according to his will, shall be beaten with many stripes.
>
> —Luke 12:47

Beloved, are you serving God today? You are responsible for that office in ministry that God has given you. Please do not abuse this God-given position as this lost soul. Be faithful till the end and you will be rewarded. If you are unfaithful like the mentioned wicked servant, you will end up being beaten with many stripes in hell.

We moved over to the next cell in much sadness. I could see a lost soul of a man. I saw huge blots of blood all over his form. He was chained and wept uncontrollably saying, "I am guilty. I am guilty."

I asked Jesus, "Lord, what is he guilty of?"

Jesus, with immense sorrow, replied, "This man is guilty of My body and blood."

"What did he do, dear Lord?" I retorted in horror.

Jesus answered, "This man, though a pastor while alive, was stubbornly persistent in a life of sin. He had no desire to give up on his sin and yet participated of My Supper willfully in an unworthy manner. Also, he did not teach his congregation not to participate of My Supper in an unworthy manner. As a shepherd of that congregation, he is responsible for this sin and is guilty of My blood and body. He has brought judgment upon himself."

> Therefore whoever eats this bread or drinks this cup of the Lord in an unworthy manner will be guilty of the body and blood of the Lord. But let a man examine himself, and so let him eat of the bread and drink of the cup. For he who eats and drinks in an unworthy manner eats and drinks judgment to himself, not discerning the Lord's body. For this reason many are weak and sick among you, and many sleep.
> —1 CORINTHIANS 11:27–30

I could see this soul lost in his own torment. Not once did he look up. In sadness, as Jesus led me away from that cell, He said, "There are many like him here."

Beloved, are you participating in the Lord's Supper and living your life in persistent sin? Beware, for you are bringing judgment upon yourself. The Lord's blood and body is not to be taken lightly. Please repent and give up that sin. Examine yourself, and then participate in the Lord's Supper. Also, if you happen to be a pastor, please warn your congregation about the dangers of participating in the Lord's Supper unworthily. As Jesus said, you are responsible as a shepherd and accountable to God for the congregation He has given you.

Chapter Thirteen

FALLEN ANGELS

*God did not spare the angels who sinned, but cast
them down to hell and delivered them into chains
of darkness, to be reserved for judgment*

—2 PETER 2:4

IN THE YEAR 2002, one afternoon in the month of May, suddenly Jesus appeared to me and said, "Daughter, come with Me." As soon as He said those words, I instantly found us inside a cavern. Jesus held my hand as we walked inside this place which was in darkness. Through the light of Jesus, I could see angels inside this cavern. Each angel appeared to be separated from another by a distance of about twenty feet. As I looked at them, I marveled at their tremendous height of what seemed much over fifteen feet. These angels did not have wings.

Jesus looked at them and said to me, "These are those angels who sinned. They took wives for themselves of all whom they chose, and hence have been reserved for judgment."

> Now it came to pass, when men began to multiply on the face of the earth, and daughters were born to them, that the sons of God saw the daughters of men, that they were beautiful; and they took wives for themselves of all whom they chose.
>
> —GENESIS 6:1–2

As I looked at the angels' faces, it appeared to me that they were remorseful of their deeds. Their once white robes appeared defiled, dirty, and torn. As I watched at a close range, one of the fallen angels suddenly appeared to look at me. I froze in fear because of his sheer height.

Then Jesus calmed my fears by saying, "Do not be afraid. They are blind and cannot see you." He gestured toward the prisoner angel's ankle. I could see that his right ankle was shackled with a leg iron. As I looked around, I saw that all those prisoner angels were shackled with leg irons in a similar fashion.

With that, I instantly found myself sitting beside Jesus inside of a noncombustible airborne object. I also noticed that there was an angel who sat with us. This airborne object emitted no sound at all, drove on its own, and traveled at a great speed upward.

As we traveled upward on our way back inside this airborne object, I noticed the dry and black earth. I also saw dry trees significantly huge in size, unlike what I have ever seen in this world. I also saw skeletal remains of a calf which was large in size, too. This was a rare glimpse of an untrodden prehistoric world.

After a while I could see houses in an alien country. As we passed by one of those houses, I could see a woman below on the terrace. It appeared to me (judging by her bewildered look) that she did notice that something flew past above her but could not make out what it was. The very next moment, I found myself back in the house. This journey seemed like a matter of minutes, though it was closer to an hour.

Chapter Fourteen

STRATEGIES OF THE ENEMY

July 2012

ONE NIGHT I was instantly translated in my spirit and found myself next to Jesus in a chamber of hell.

Jesus said to me, "Daughter, it is here that Satan holds important discussions related to his kingdom and also plans his attacks against My children. I have brought you here to listen to his schemes and warn My people." I understood then that this was that chamber Jesus had told me about earlier, where He would bring me when it was in operation (see Satan's Conference Chamber in chapter 10).

I could see Satan and his demons involved in a series of discussion. We moved closer and stood right behind them. As Satan spoke, those powerful demons listened attentively. This is what I heard Satan say: "I created the religions of the world to keep them [mankind] away from Him [God]. Humanity belongs to me. There are many who attend churches but are still mine [he said this with a hideous laughter]. He [Jesus] came and destroyed my plans and snatched them [mankind] away from me. I will destroy those who belong to Him [Jesus]."

Speaking with immense anger, hatred, and frustration, he commanded in an urgent tone, "Tighten the noose around this flock [referring to real Christians]. These are the arrogant ones who refuse to worship me. Do everything in your power to make them lose their zeal for Him [Jesus]. Thus, I will retain my worship in their lives and He [God] will be defeated. Destroy those who refuse to worship me. We will achieve our purpose through His [God's] creation [referring to man] and destroy them. Man will kill man; more bloodshed; more killings. [Satan urged his demons to do the same.] We do not have much time. Plunder as many as possible. [He said this in regard to souls.] We will take the maximum with us [referring to his punishment in hell outlined in Revelation 20:10]. This will be our victory against Him [God]. But before that happens, my worship will be established on earth."

Beloved, just as he said, Satan created the religions to keep mankind from the one true God. He knows man is doomed to hell if he fails to share a living relationship with God through His Son Jesus Christ. Satan also knows that his time is running out. His schemes and plans revolved around destruction of mankind in an attempt to get even with God, establish worship of himself, and to dethrone God and enthrone himself.

Satan hates man created in God's own image (Gen. 1:27). Satan was thrown out of heaven and he resents the fact that God created mankind to share an intimate relationship with Him and also inherit great and precious promises by being partakers of divine nature.

> His divine power has given to us all things that pertain
> to life and godliness, through the knowledge of Him who
> called us by glory and virtue, by which have been given to
> us exceedingly great and precious promises, that through
> these you may be partakers of the divine nature.
>
> —2 Peter 1:3–4

Because of this, Satan planned the fall of mankind. Yet God in His abundant love and mercy made a way for us to return back to Him through Jesus Christ, who Himself became the propitiation of our sins.

> In this is love, not that we loved God, but that He loved us
> and sent His Son to be the propitiation for our sins.
>
> —1 John 4:10

And He restores our estranged relationship with God such that we call Him Abba, Father. "And because you are sons, God has sent forth the Spirit of His Son into your hearts, crying out, 'Abba, Father!'" (Gal. 4:6).

The world lies under the sway of the wicked one. The enemy has and will attempt to blind the eyes of gullible souls by deviating them from this truth and offering them an alternative path to their destruction in the form of religion. Religion is a deliberate attempt by the enemy to keep mankind away from the saving knowledge of Jesus Christ. As Satan said, religions were created by him. If you are following a religion instead of sharing a relationship with Jesus Christ in spirit and truth, you are blinded and deceived by the enemy.

> Whose minds the god of this age has blinded, who do not believe, lest the light of the gospel of the glory of Christ, who is the image of God, should shine on them.
> —2 Corinthians 4:4

You might even be a Christian and trying to reach God through your own means. Beloved, religion saves no one; you need to be born again to go to heaven. Please repent and form a relationship with your Creator before it is too late. God wants to be a Father to you.

> "I will be a Father to you, And you shall be My sons and daughters," says the Lord Almighty.
> —2 Corinthians 6:18

Unless this becomes a reality in your life, you are lost. You can be attending a church and on your way to hell.

Satan is engaged in all-out war against real Christians—those who live by the Word of God and do not compromise. These are the ones he referred to as "the flock." This flock is a minority, no doubt, in this predominantly evil world, yet it is powerful enough to mess up his plans.

Beloved, if you are a practicing Christian, get prepared to be tested for your faith like never before. Satan is tightening his noose around real Christians, as he said. He will do everything in his power to significantly increase the severity of his attacks as days go by and before darkness settles in this world. If you do not take a stand for your beliefs, you will be pulled in by the lies and deceptions of the enemy.

The Word of God is the truth, and you cannot afford to compromise on this truth. As a Christian you are called not just to know this truth but also to love this truth. If you fail to do this, it will result in your spiritual ruin "with all unrighteous deception among those who perish, because they did not receive the love of the truth, that they might be saved" (2 Thess. 2:10).

When you begin to compromise, you also begin to lose your passion and zeal for Jesus Christ. This passivity gradually results in unfruitfulness toward God's work. Satan pointed out this fact in his conversation with demons. Hence, he tries hard to make you compromise.

Beloved, do not reestablish Satan's throne in your life that God has dethroned. Jesus said, "The ruler of this world is coming, and he has nothing in Me" (John 14:30).

Reader, do you have any part of Satan in your life? Remember, if you have any part of Satan in your life, you are still worshipping him. He longs to establish his throne in your life so that you will worship him. Hence, do not give any place to the devil in your life.

Satan's purposeful attack on and suppression of biblical beliefs and values will increase in the coming days. Get ready for an intense battle. You will be nailed for speaking the truth and standing up for God: "And you will be hated by all for My name's sake. But he who endures to the end shall be saved" (Mark 13:13).

As days go by, distortion of the Scripture and unbiblical beliefs will be promoted in the open like never before and also approved.

Spiritual decay will thrive. Make sure that your love for God does not grow cold.

> The time will come when they will not endure sound doctrine, but according to their own desires, because they have itching ears, they will heap up for themselves teachers; and they will turn their ears away from the truth, and be turned aside to fables.
>
> —2 TIMOTHY 4:3–4

> Being filled with all unrighteousness, sexual immorality, wickedness, covetousness, maliciousness; full of envy, murder, strife, deceit, evil-mindedness; they are whisperers, backbiters, haters of God, violent, proud, boasters, inventors of evil things, disobedient to parents, undiscerning, untrustworthy, unloving, unforgiving, unmerciful; who, knowing the righteous judgment of God, that those who practice such things are deserving of death, not only do the same but also approve of those who practice them.
>
> —ROMANS 1:29–32

Beloved, we are engaged in a fierce battle waged by the enemy and the power of the enemy cannot be underestimated. Not unaware of his schemes, let us "put on the whole armor of God, that you may be able to stand against the wiles of the devil" (Eph. 6:11). This armor of God works effectively when you walk in holiness and truth. The enemy backs off only after seeing the truth in your life. Satan wishes, wants, and plans purposefully for the destruction of mankind whom God so lovingly created with His hands and in His image (Gen. 1:27). His hatred for mankind—God's creation—is such that in their destruction he seeks to avenge himself of what he has been deprived of and his doom by God. Hence, he views his attempt to destroy mankind as an attack on God Himself.

The purposeful violent acts of massacre in human history till date bear witness of his destruction. Satan uses people, just as he said "man will kill man"—whoever is willing and open to be used of him, to achieve and assist in his purpose of destruction of mankind. Apart from all wickedness, murder in any form—whether abortions, acts of terrorism, etc.—is powered and instigated by the enemy. I heard him urge those demons for more bloodshed and more killing, and in the coming days killings will increase significantly. Many times I witnessed demons go berserk over human blood. To kill humans thrills the enemy and gives them an occasion to celebrate. The Bible calls Satan a murderer: "He was a murderer from the beginning, and does not stand in the truth, because there is no truth in him" (John 8:44). He comes to rob, steal, kill, and destroy: "The thief does not come except to steal, and to kill, and to destroy" (John 10:10).

Beloved, come to Jesus before the darkness settles in this world. Unless the salvation of Jesus Christ is a reality and a testimony in your life, you cannot overcome the enemy.

> And they overcame him by the blood of the Lamb and by the word of their testimony, and they did not love their lives to the death.
>
> —REVELATION 12:11

Chapter Fifteen

WALKING OUT OF THE GATES OF HELL

August 2012

"WE ARE LEAVING this place now." This is what Jesus said to me on my last visit to hell. As we walked past those cells and pits, amidst the groaning and the wailings of the lost, I was relieved inside that never again would I have to step into this dreadful place of gloom and terror.

Suddenly it appeared as if the lost could see me. With their blackened, burned, and folded skeletal hands and tears that appeared irrespective of empty sockets that streamed down their burned faces and then disappeared, they screamed in desperate high-pitched tones: "Please warn our families! Please tell them not to come here!" Their shrill voices echoed in my ears. Their desperate, painful pleas rang inside of me as we continued to walk toward the high black gate, which Jesus referred to as the way out of hell.

Now instead of relief, I walked with a heavy heart amidst their pleadings. I realized that I could walk out of this gate of hell but they, the imprisoned, were the eternal captives here. As we exited out of this place, the black high gate promptly shut behind us. Unable to contain my sadness, I sobbed right outside that black gate.

After letting me sob awhile, Jesus looked at me tenderly and said with much compassion, "Daughter, do I have any pleasure at all that the wicked should die? And not that he should turn from his ways and live? (Ezek. 18:23). This is the reason I have shown you the horror of hell. Warn the world that hell is real."

As I write this, the cries and the pleas of the condemned echo in my ears. I am unable to forget their tears that streamed down and then disappeared on their burned faces. Their blackened skeleton forms and their eternal affliction haunt me.

I urge you to please turn from your wicked ways. Hell is awfully real. I may not know you personally, yet will not want you to go there. Repent and accept Jesus in your life. Make heaven your destination, not hell.

Chapter Sixteen

JESUS WEEPS

A FTER SPEAKING THOSE words, suddenly Jesus began to weep. It was distressing to see my Lord weep, and I enquired as to what was troubling Him. I reckoned within myself that He wept because of the lost souls.

After a moment of silence, Jesus looked at me and said in a choked voice, "Daughter, I weep for My body [meaning the church]. Over those who do not repent and will end up here [pointing toward the gates of hell]. 'It is written My house is a house of prayer but these people have made it a den of thieves' (Luke 19:46). They have sold Me in exchange for the world and its allurements. Warn them, before it is too late!"

Then Jesus began to explain to me the three specific types of Christians found in the church today He was gravely concerned and distressed about and wept for.

Compromising Christians

The first type of those Christians Jesus mentioned are the compromising Christians.

The term *compromise* refers to settlement of differences by mutual concessions. In a Christian, however, this compromise takes place at the cost of our convictions. The act of compromise usually stems from loving the world and the things in it. The Bible strictly prohibits us to love the world.

> Do not love the world or the things in the world. If any one loves the world, the love of the Father is not in him. For

all that is in the world—the lust of the flesh, the lust of the eyes, and the pride of life—is not of the Father but is of the world.

—1 JOHN 2:15–16

In doing so we make ourselves an enemy of God.

Adulterers and adulteresses! Do you not know that friendship with the world is enmity with God? Whoever therefore wants to be a friend of the world makes himself an enemy of God.

—JAMES 4:4

This was Satan's final bait in his attempt to entice Jesus.

Again, the devil took Him up on an exceedingly high mountain, and showed Him all the kingdoms of the world and their glory. And he said to Him, "All these things I will give You if You will fall down and worship me."

—MATTHEW 4:8–9

Therefore, to compromise is to fall from biblical beliefs and convictions for the gratification of "the lust of the flesh, the lust of the eyes, and the pride of life" (1 John 2:16).

This eventually brings forth death.

But each one is tempted when he is drawn away by his own desires and enticed. Then, when desire has conceived, it gives birth to sin; and sin, when it is full-grown, brings forth death.

—JAMES 1:14–15

Jesus also spoke to me regarding the three areas of compromise within the church that are causing extensive damage to the body of Christ.

1. Perversion of Scripture

> All Scripture is given by inspiration of God, and is profit-
> able for doctrine, for reproof, for correction, for instruction
> in righteousness.
>
> —2 Timothy 3:16

God's Word is the absolute inerrant truth, and therefore cannot
be compromised for any reason or anyone. There are some in the
body of Christ who add or subtract, handle the Word of God deceit-
fully, or twist it to suit their own selfish purposes and in a bid to
please the crowd. The Bible warns against:

a. Addition or subtraction

> You shall not add to the word which I command you, nor
> take from it, that you may keep the commandments of the
> Lord your God which I command you.
>
> —Deuteronomy 4:2

b. Deceitful handling

> But we have renounced the hidden things of shame, not
> walking in craftiness nor handling the word of God deceit-
> fully, but by manifestation of the truth commending our-
> selves to every man's conscience in the sight of God.
>
> —2 Corinthians 4:2

c. Twisting for personal benefit

> As also in all his epistles, speaking in them of these things,
> in which are some things hard to understand, which
> untaught and unstable people twist to their own destruc-
> tion, as they do also the rest of the Scriptures.
>
> —2 Peter 3:16

d. Invalidating by traditions

Also, there are some who place their traditions that have been passed down to them through generations above the Word of God and make it ineffective.

> He said to them, "All too well you reject the commandment of God, that you may keep your tradition. For Moses said, 'Honor your father and your mother'; and, 'He who curses father or mother, let him be put to death.' But you say, 'If a man says to his father or mother, "Whatever profit you might have received from me is Corban"—' (that is, a gift to God), then you no longer let him do anything for his father or his mother, making the word of God of no effect through your tradition which you have handed down. And many such things you do."
>
> —MARK 7:9–13

We have been brought forth through this Word of truth.

> Of His own will He brought us forth by the word of truth, that we might be a kind of firstfruits of His creatures.
>
> —JAMES 1:18

Ministers of God, please preach the truth as it is, for its purity results in birthing new life, and do not seek to please the secular world.

> For do I now persuade men, or God? Or do I seek to please men? For if I still pleased men, I would not be a bondservant of Christ.
>
> —GALATIANS 1:10

> But has now been revealed by the appearing of our Savior Jesus Christ, who has abolished death and brought life and immortality to light through the gospel.
>
> —2 TIMOTHY 1:10

Dilution of the purity of God's Word amounts to sacrilege. The convicting power of the gospel lies in its truth. Turning away from the truth in an attempt to please the crowd strips off its effectiveness and renders it equivalent to fables.

> But the time will come when they will not endure sound doctrine, but according to their own desires, because they have itching ears, they will heap up for themselves teachers; and they will turn their ears away from the truth, and be turn aside to fables.
>
> —2 Timothy 4:3–4

It is important to receive the love of the truth to be saved. In the absence of truth, spiritual decay thrives and leads to destruction.

> For the wrath of God is revealed from heaven against all ungodliness and unrighteousness of men, who suppress the truth in unrighteousness.
>
> —Romans 1:18

Reader, if you have erred from the truth of the Word of God, please repent. The Bible commands us to "hold fast to the truth" (Titus 1:9) and speak this truth whether in season or out of season.

> Preach the Word; be prepared in season and out of season; correct, rebuke and encourage—with great patience and careful instruction.
>
> —2 Timothy 4:2, NIV

2. Marriage

Jesus spoke with much sadness about those Christians who compromise in marrying unbelievers much against the teachings of His Word. The Bible warns us not to be unequally yoked with unbelievers.

> Do not be unequally yoked together with unbelievers. For what fellowship has righteousness with lawlessness? And what communion has light with darkness? And what accord has Christ with Belial? Or what part has a believer with an unbeliever? And what agreement has the temple of God with idols? For you are the temple of the living God. As God has said: "I will dwell in them And walk among them. I will be their God, And they shall be My people."
> —2 CORINTHIANS 6:14–16

Marriage to an unbeliever results in (a) unequal yoking, (b) fellowship with lawlessness, (c) communion with darkness, (d) accord with Belial, and (e) an agreement with idols.

As a born-again Christian, you are the temple of the living God, and marrying an unbeliever is a treacherous abomination that profanes the Lord's holy institution of marriage. I met a lost soul of a woman in hell who had married an idol worshipper and ended up in hell (mentioned in chapter 12). Jesus said to her, "You profaned My institution of marriage."

Beloved, to marry an unbeliever is to incite God's wrath and this follows with a curse as a punishment.

> Judah has dealt treacherously, and an abomination has been committed in Israel and in Jerusalem, For Judah has profaned the LORD's holy institution which He loves: He has married the daughter of a foreign god. May the LORD cut off from the tents of Jacob the man who does this, being awake and aware, yet who brings an offering to the LORD of hosts!
> —MALACHI 2:11–12

Beloved, this kind of union is without God's blessing. Please do not be unequally yoked with unbelievers in marriage. Have a God blessed and God ordained marriage. With marriage, you become one flesh with your spouse; and it is sacrilege to be one with an idol worshipper since you are the temple of the Holy Spirit and not your own.

> Do you not know that your body is the temple of the Holy Spirit who is in you, whom you have from God, and you are not your own.
>
> —1 CORINTHIANS 6:19

If you are joined to the Lord, you are one spirit with Him. "But he who is joined to the Lord is one spirit with Him" (1 Cor. 6:17). Therefore, the temple of God cannot have any agreement with the idols. It is a treacherous sin and strictly prohibited in the Bible.

The Word of God records that King Solomon's foreign wives turned his heart away from God to idolatry and his heart was not loyal to God. There are many who hope in vain that their spouse will convert after marriage. Deciding to marry an unbeliever based on this hope is unwise. Moreover, this is in direct disobedience to the Word and will result in serious implications in your personal walk with Christ.

> But King Solomon loved many foreign women…from the nations of whom the LORD had said to the children of Israel, "You shall not intermarry with them, nor they with you. Surely they will turn away your hearts after their gods." Solomon clung to these in love….For it was so, when Solomon was old, that his wives turned his heart after other gods; and his heart was not loyal to the LORD his God.
>
> —1 KINGS 11:1–2, 4

An important purpose of God in marriage is to produce godly seed.

> But did He not make them one, Having a remnant of the Spirit? And why one? He seeks godly offspring. Therefore take heed to your spirit.
>
> —MALACHI 2:15

If you have compromised in marriage, please repent and make a decision to serve God wholeheartedly.

> And if it seems evil to you to serve the LORD, choose for yourselves this day whom you will serve, whether the gods which your fathers served that were on the other side of the River, or the gods of the Amorites, in whose land you dwell. But as for me and my house, we will serve the LORD.
>
> —JOSHUA 24:15

Remember, your blessing depends on the decision you make. It is conditional. If you repent, there is hope in Jesus Christ regarding your family. He will sanctify your unbelieving spouse and make your children holy.

> For the unbelieving husband is sanctified by the wife, and the unbelieving wife is sanctified by the husband otherwise your children would be unclean, but now they are holy.
>
> —1 CORINTHIANS 7:14

3. Sexual immorality

Jesus went on to speak about those in the body of Christ who are practicing double lives—outwardly Christians yet deeply immersed in sexual immorality. If you are a person under the bondage of any form of sexual perversion, whether adultery, fornication, homosexuality, incest, pornography, etc., please repent and renounce your sin.

> For this is the will of God, your sanctification: that you should abstain from sexual immorality; that each of you should know how to possess his own vessel in sanctification and honor not in passion of lust, like the Gentiles who do not know God....For God did not call us to uncleanness, but in holiness. Therefore he who rejects this does not reject man, but God, who has also given us His Holy Spirit.
>
> —1 THESSALONIANS 4:3–5, 7–8

Beloved, to live in sexual immorality is to reject God, as mentioned above. God accepts you as you are and forgives you, like the woman caught in adultery to whom Jesus said, "Neither do I condemn you, go and sin no more" (John 8:11).

He expects you to renounce your sin. You might be serving God in ministry yet be a slave to sexual immorality and living in sin. Repent now while there is time. If you were to die in this sin, you will end up in hell.

I beheld several lost souls in hell; some had even served God in ministry while leading double lives. They had believed that they would not end up in hell since they were serving God. But they realized after their death that they were deceived.

> Do not be deceived, God is not to be mocked, for what a man sows so shall he reap. For he who sows to his flesh will of the flesh reap corruption but he who sows to the Spirit will of the Spirit reap everlasting life.
>
> —GALATIANS 6:7–8

God does not compromise the standard of His Word for any reason or anyone: "For you have magnified Your word above all Your name" (Ps. 138:2). To be holy is a command and not an option: "Be holy, for I am holy" (1 Pet. 1:16).

Therefore, purge out that addiction that leavens the whole lump and be an example to the believers and nonbelievers alike "in word, in conduct, in love, in spirit, in faith, in purity" (1 Tim. 4:12); and keep the feast with the unleavened bread of sincerity and truth.

> Do you not know that a little leaven leavens the whole lump? Therefore purge out the old leaven, that you may be a new lump, since you truly are unleavened. For indeed Christ, our Passover, was sacrificed for us. Therefore let us keep the feast, not with old leaven, nor with the leaven of malice and wickedness, but with the unleavened bread of sincerity and truth.
>
> —1 CORINTHIANS 5:6–8

Sexual immorality brings you under bondage: "By whom a person is overcome, by him also he is brought into bondage" (2 Pet. 2:19). You need to be set free from this bondage of sin: "Therefore whom the Son of God sets free is free indeed" (John 8:36).

Please repent today while grace abounds in Jesus Christ. Now is the time to repent.

> And I gave her time to repent of her sexual immorality, and she did not repent. Indeed I will cast her into a sickbed, and those who commit adultery with her into great tribulation, unless they repent of their deeds. I will kill her children with death, and all the churches shall know that I am He who searches the minds and hearts. And I will give to each one of you according to your works.
> —REVELATION 2:21–23

In the hour of temptation, let your response be that of Jesus: "Away with you Satan!" (Matt. 4:10). Begin to treat older men as fathers, "younger men as brothers, older women as mothers, younger women as sisters, with all purity" (1 Tim. 5:1–2). "He who has ears to hear, let him hear!" (Matt. 11:15).

Self-righteous Christians

The boastful, self-centered, and righteous in their own eyes ardently following the traditions—the fear of God taught by precepts of men handed down from past generations yet their hearts are far away from God—is the second category of those Christians Jesus weeps for and asked me to warn.

Self-righteousness originates through trust on oneself and is dependent on works. Biblically, self-righteousness arises from not submitting to God's righteousness.

> For they being ignorant of God's righteousness, and seeking to establish their own righteousness, have not submitted to the righteousness of God.
> —ROMANS 10:3

God equates acts of self-righteousness to filthy rags: "But we are all like an unclean thing, And all our righteousness are like filthy rags" (Isa. 64:6).

On the other hand, righteousness originates through the grace of God by faith in Christ.

> That I may gain Christ and be found in Him, not having my own righteousness which is from the law, but that which is through faith in Christ, the righteousness which is from God by faith.
>
> —Philippians 3:8–9

Jesus explains this clearly in His example of the Pharisee and the tax collector:

> Also He spoke this parable to some who trusted in themselves that they were righteous, and despised others: "Two men went up to the temple to pray, one a Pharisee and the other a tax collector. The Pharisee stood and prayed thus with himself, 'God, I thank You that I am not like other men—extortioners, unjust, adulterers, or even as this tax collector. I fast twice a week; I give tithes of all that I possess.' And the tax collector, standing afar off, would not so much as raise his eyes to heaven, but beat his breast, saying, 'God, be merciful to me a sinner!' I tell you, this man went down to his house justified rather than the other; for everyone who exalts himself will be humbled, and he who humbles himself will be exalted."
>
> —Luke 18:9–14

The Pharisee mentioned here was walking according to the tradition of the fathers and was zealous for them no doubt. As he carefully details his self-righteous acts, displaying his pride of justification, he is also very aware of the sins of others, including the tax collector, and views them with contempt. Trusting in his self-righteous acts, he expects to obtain merit from God, completely unaware that God rejected him outright.

> Woe to you, scribes and Pharisees, hypocrites! For you pay tithe of mint and anise and cumin, and have neglected the weightier matters of the law: justice and mercy and faith. These you ought to have done, without leaving the others undone. Blind guides, who strain out a gnat and swallow a camel!
>
> —MATTHEW 23:23–24

Meanwhile, the tax collector, sorry for his sins, acknowledges humbly that he is a sinner and hence obtains God's mercy.

The Pharisee's self-righteous acts were rooted in tradition. He had simply carried out those acts that he had been taught that were passed down to him from his fathers and he knew as tradition. His fear of God was taught by men: "Their fear toward Me is taught by the commandment of men" (Isa. 29:13). God terms this as vain worship, and hence, it is unacceptable to Him. "And in vain they worship Me, Teaching as doctrines the commandments of men" (Matt. 15:9).

Tradition is inconsistent with Christ.

> Beware lest anyone cheat you through philosophy and empty deceit, according to the tradition of men, according to the basic principles of the world, and not according to Christ.
>
> —COLOSSIANS 2:8

Tradition results in three things:

1. Aimless conduct

> You were not redeemed with…your aimless conduct received by tradition from your fathers.
>
> —1 PETER 1:18

2. Hypocrisy

Well did Isaiah prophesy of you hypocrites, as it is written: "This people honors Me with their lips, But their heart is far from Me."

—MARK 7:6

3. Rejection of God's Word

Laying aside the commandment of God, you hold the tradition of men—the washing of pitchers and cups, and many other such things you do.

—MARK 7:8

Tradition is a man-made attempt to try to reach God and appease Him. Beloved, your self-righteous acts can never remove the stain of your sin. You need to be cleansed internally. The consequence of sin is so serious that it attracts a death penalty. "The wages of sin is death" (Rom. 6:23).

To save you and me, Jesus Christ Himself took our place on the cross for our sins and redeemed us with His blood. "In Him we have redemption through His blood, the forgiveness of sins, according to the riches of His grace" (Eph. 1:7).

Self-righteousness discounts sin, which is punishable by death, and nullifies the work of Jesus Christ on the cross making it meaningless. Beloved, self-righteousness results in rejecting the salvation that God, in His love and mercy, offers as a gift. "The gift of God is eternal life in Christ Jesus our Lord" (Rom. 6:23).

The self-righteous Pharisee in the above-mentioned parable was blinded to spiritual things. Beloved, if you let tradition—commandments of men—take precedence over God's Word, you will be blinded to spiritual things like this Pharisee was.

> Because you say, "I am rich, have become wealthy, and have need of nothing"—and do not know that you are wretched, miserable, poor, blind, and naked—I counsel you to buy

from Me gold refined in the fire, that you may be rich; and white garments, that you may be clothed, that the shame of your nakedness may not be revealed; and anoint your eyes with eye salve, that you may see.

—REVELATION 3:17–18

You are wretched, miserable, poor, blind, and naked if you are not born again, without which you will by no means enter the kingdom of heaven. Acts of self-righteousness or following traditions saves no one.

For I say to you, that unless your righteousness exceeds the righteousness of the scribes and Pharisees, you will by no means enter the kingdom of heaven.

—MATTHEW 5:20

In His conversation with Nicodemus, Jesus emphasized the necessity of being born again to see the kingdom of God.

There was a man of the Pharisees named Nicodemus, a ruler of the Jews. This man came to Jesus by night and said to Him, "Rabbi, we know that You are a teacher come from God; for no one can do these signs that You do unless God is with him." Jesus answered and said to him, "Most assuredly, I say to you, unless one is born again, he cannot see the kingdom of God." Nicodemus said to Him, "How can a man be born when he is old? Can he enter a second time into his mother's womb and be born?" Jesus answered, "Most assuredly, I say to you, unless one is born of water and the Spirit, he cannot enter the kingdom of God. That which is born of the flesh is flesh, and that which is born of the Spirit is spirit. Do not marvel that I said to you, 'You must be born again.'"

—JOHN 3:1–7

Salvation comes by grace through faith in Jesus Christ.

> For by grace you have been saved through faith, and that
> not of yourselves; it is the gift of God, not of by works, lest
> anyone should boast.
>
> —EPHESIANS 2:8–9

Salvation cannot be earned by self-righteous works. It is the work of God. In fact, the only work you must do is desire to be saved. Jesus answered and said to them, "This is the work of God, that you believe in Him whom He sent" (John 6:29). You need to come to the saving knowledge of Jesus Christ today. Repent and be saved.

I beheld many lost souls in hell who thought salvation could be earned through works. These were deceived by the enemy into believing that following the traditions of the church would land them in heaven.

Beloved, are you born again? Do you share a personal relationship with God? If not, then seek to do this right away. Is your relationship with Christ limited to religion? Are you trying to reach Him by adhering to tradition? If Christianity is limited to being a religion to you, then you are lost.

You might be highly respected today in the society, boast of your charitable deeds, and consider yourself important, yet be unsaved. No matter what you testify of yourself, it is of most importance what God has to say about you.

This is what God said about Pharisees:

> These people draw near with their mouths And honor Me
> with their lips, But have removed their hearts far from Me,
> And their fear toward Me is taught by the commandment
> of men.
>
> —ISAIAH 29:13

As for Jesus, God testified, "This is My Beloved Son in whom I am well pleased. Listen to Him" (Matt. 17:5, NIV).

Beloved, what is your testimony today? Does God testify in your favor or against you? "For not he who commends himself is approved, but whom the Lord commends" (2 Cor. 10:18). Similar to the tax collector, humbly acknowledge and admit that you are a sinner and you need to be born again. This humility will help you find grace with God.

> As many as I love, I rebuke and chasten. Therefore be zealous and repent. Behold, I stand at the door and knock. If anyone hears My voice and opens the door, I will come in to him and dine with him, and he with Me.
> —REVELATION 3:19–20

Make sure you get on God's side by being born again today when you have this opportunity: "Today is the day of salvation" (2 Cor. 6:2, NLT). It will be too late after death.

Asleep Christians

The third category of Christians Jesus weeps over comprises those unregenerate Christians who are asleep and lost in the slumber of wickedness. You might call yourself a Christian but well be in a perpetual sleep in a life of sin. Though you are much alive in your body, you are dead spiritually and unable to perceive and understand the things of God.

The Word of God says that we are neither of the night nor of darkness. Let us not sleep but let us watch and be sober.

> You are all sons of light and sons of the day. We are not of the night nor of darkness. Therefore let us not sleep, as others do, but let us watch and be sober. For those who sleep, sleep at night, and those who get drunk are drunk at night.
> —1 THESSALONIANS 5:5–7

While sleep can be defined as the state of complete or partial unconsciousness, here it is speaking of the spirit and results in causing insensitivity to the spiritual things of God. The darkness and its associated wicked deeds bring about this sleep. This sleep originates from walking in the futility of the mind.

> This I say, therefore, and testify in the Lord, that you should no longer walk as the rest of the Gentiles walk, in the futility of their mind, having their understanding darkened, being alienated from the life of God, because of the ignorance that is in them.
> —Ephesians 4:17–18

> And you He made alive, who were dead in trespasses and sins, in which you once walked according to the by course of this world, according to the prince of the power of the air, the spirit who now works in the sons of disobedience, among whom also we all once conducted ourselves in the lusts of our flesh, fulfilling the desires of the flesh and of the mind, and were by nature children of wrath, just as the others.
> —Ephesians 2:1–3

Paul is warning us to no longer walk "according to the prince of the power of air, the spirit who now works in the sons of disobedience" (Eph. 2:2).

People of corrupt nature live solely by setting their affections on the carnal satisfaction of the "lust of the eyes, the lust of the flesh, and the pride of life which is not of the Father but of the world" (1 John 2:16). As a result of not being born of the new nature that comes from God, they live a life much in opposite to God's divine nature and His principles of standard laid out in His Word to live righteously. Naturally, because of their carnal nature, not only do they deem those things that appeal to them to be good but they also provide for them with gusto. The sins of the flesh are evident:

> And even as they did not like to retain God in their knowledge, God gave them over to a debased mind, to do those things which are not fitting; being filled with all

unrighteousness, sexual immorality, wickedness, covetous-
ness, maliciousness; full of envy, murder, strife, deceit, evil-
mindedness; they are whisperers, backbiters, haters of God,
violent, proud, boasters, inventors of evil things, disobe-
dient to parents, undiscerning, untrustworthy, unloving,
unforgiving, unmerciful; who, knowing the righteous
judgment of God, that those who practice such things are
deserving of death, not only do the same but also approve
of those who practice them.

—ROMANS 1:28–32

This perpetual walk in sin results in the following three points:

1. Darkness of understanding

Hearing you will hear and shall not understand, And seeing
you will see and not perceive.

—MATTHEW 13:14

Sin separates man from God and perverts his thinking to an
effect that "nothing is pure; even their mind and conscience are
defiled" (Titus 1:15). As a result of this darkness, the person does
not have the understanding to meditate on things which are true,
noble, just, pure, lovely, good report, with virtue, or praiseworthy
(Phil. 4:8). The veil of sin darkens the understanding and therefore "he who walks in darkness does not know where he is going"
(John 12:35).

2. Slavery to sin

If you present yourself as an instrument of unrighteousness to
sin, it will have dominion over you and make you its slave.

Do you not know that to whom you present yourselves
slaves to obey, you are that one's slaves whom you obey,

whether of sin leading to death, or of obedience leading to righteousness?

—ROMANS 6:16

This is the reason Jesus said, "He who commits sin is a slave of sin" (John 8:34). Do not participate in sin mistaking it as casual, something you are in control of, and something you can get out of anytime.

Beloved, unless you repent and renounce that sin, there is no way you can come out of it. Sin is gripping; and once you are caught in its tentacles, there is no escaping. No matter what the addiction—whether drugs, illicit sex, pornography, etc.—once you have given yourself to sin, it begins to control you.

This slavery of sin leads to the third point:

3. Blindness of heart

The blind slaves of sensuality continue in persistent sinning without regret, and they eventually lose all moral sensitivity. They have given themselves to lewdness in their overwhelming need for carnal gratification of shameful impurity that needs to be satisfied at any cost and anyhow with a continual greed for more. This explains the crimes that take place crossing moral boundaries.

> Having their understanding darkened, being alienated from the life of God, because of the ignorance that is in them, because of the blindness of their heart; who, being past feeling, have given themselves over to lewdness, to work all uncleanness with greediness.
>
> —EPHESIANS 4:18–19

As a result of habitual sinning and not paying heed to godly discipline, the conscience of the person is eventually destroyed, as if it were seared with a hot iron.

> Some will depart from the faith giving heed to deceiving
> spirits and doctrines of demons, speaking lies in hypocrisy,
> having their own conscience seared with a hot iron.
>
> —1 TIMOTHY 4:1–2

As a result, the person is not able to ascertain right from wrong. Being "dead in trespasses and sins" (Eph. 2:1) makes one spiritually blinded to the things of God; in other words, "asleep." Those in this state are by nature the children of wrath, "enemies of God" (Col. 1:21), and alienated from the life of God and deserving punishment. "For to be carnally minded is death" (Rom. 8:6).

Beloved, have the things of the world and its sensual allurements taken precedence over God in your life? Overtaken by the heaviness of slumber, are you sunk in the depths of sin—physically alive but spiritually dead? Are you in this state today? If so, then this sleep is your ticket to hell.

Awake before it is too late. If you were to die in this state, you will surely end up in hell. God is calling you to an essential spiritual awakening. Therefore, "awake, you who sleep, Arise from the dead And Christ will give you light" (Eph. 5:14).

There is only one provision that can shed light in your spiritual darkness—Jesus Christ. No matter how blinded you are to God, He will open your eyes.

> Open their eyes, in order to turn them from darkness to
> light, and from the power of Satan to God, that they may
> receive forgiveness of sins and an inheritance among those
> who are sanctified by faith in Me.
>
> —ACTS 26:18

Therefore, beloved:

a. Repent and be saved,

> For it pleased the Father that in Him all the fullness should
> dwell, and by Him to reconcile all things to Himself, by

Him, whether things on earth or things in heaven, having
made peace through the blood of His cross.

—Colossians 1:19–20

b. Cast off the works of darkness,

The night is far spent, the day is at hand. Therefore let us
cast off the works of darkness, and let us put on the armor
of light.

—Romans 13:12

c. Let your walk be pleasing to God,

Let us walk properly, as in the day, not in revelry and
drunkenness, not in lewdness and lust, not in strife and
envy.

—Romans 13:13

d. Put on the Lord Jesus Christ,

But put on the Lord Jesus Christ, and make no provision
for the flesh, to fulfill its lusts.

—Romans 13:14

e. And be filled with the Holy Spirit.

Be filled with the Spirit.

—Ephesians 5:18

The Holy Spirit of God helps us to lead a holy life in this sinful
world. So seek to be filled with His Spirit.

You might be a Christian who was saved once, but now are lost
in the slumber of sin. Do not be deceived by the enemy that you
will still make it to heaven even if you were to die in this sinful
state.

Beloved, you will not make it to heaven if you do not repent.

The Bible says, "There is therefore now no condemnation to those who are in Christ Jesus, *who do not walk according to the flesh, but according to the Spirit*" (Rom. 8:1, emphasis added). Therefore, wake up from that slumber of sin and live!

Do you identify with any of the above-mentioned Christians? Jesus weeps over you. Please repent and turn back to God and become sons of light while His light is still around.

> While you have the light, believe in the light, that you may become sons of light.
>
> —John 12:36

Chapter Seventeen

JESUS IS COMING VERY SOON!

R<small>IGHT AFTER JESUS</small> spoke about the three categories of Christians who cause Him immense anguish and grief, I suddenly found us on the clouds surrounded by angels. My attention was drawn to one particular archangel who held a trumpet to his mouth ready to blow the trumpet any minute to announce the return of the Lord Jesus Christ.

As I trembled in awe to see such a sight, Jesus looked at me and said, "Daughter, I am coming very soon—much sooner than you think. I am coming for a holy and spotless bride without blemish. Warn My people to be prepared for My return."

Beloved, it is imperative to be prepared for the second coming of the Lord Jesus Christ. He will appear either for the joy of His children or the mourning of the wicked. If you are prepared for the day of His return, you will rejoice; and if you are not prepared, you will mourn. Make sure that you are found among those who will rejoice on His return.

> Then the sign of the Son of Man will appear in heaven, and then all the tribes of the earth will mourn, and they will see the Son of Man coming on the clouds of heaven with power and great glory. And He will send His angels with a great sound of a trumpet, and they will gather together His elect from the four winds, from one end of heaven to the other.
> —MATTHEW 24:30–31

The Bible describes the return of the Lord Jesus Christ as a thief in the night and as the days of Noah.

But the day of the Lord will come as a thief in the night, in which the heavens will pass away with a great noise, and the elements will melt with fervent heat; both the earth and the works that are in it will be burned up.

—2 Peter 3:10

But as the days of Noah were, so also will the coming of the Son of Man be. For as in the days before the flood, they were eating and drinking, marrying and giving in marriage, until the day that Noah entered the ark, and did not know until the flood came and took them all away, so also will the coming of the Son of Man be. Then two men will be in the field: one will be taken and the other left. Two women will be grinding at the mill: one will be taken and the other left. Watch therefore, for you do not know what hour your Lord is coming.

—Matthew 24:37–42

And on His return, He will sit on the throne of His glory.

When the Son of Man comes in His glory, and all the holy angels with Him, then He will sit on the throne of His glory.

—Matthew 25:31

As His precious children eagerly awaiting His revelation, let us come short in no gift so that we may be blameless at His coming. Beloved, let us do the following:

1. Walk worthy of our calling.

Denying ungodliness and worldly lusts, we should live soberly, righteously, and godly in the present age, looking for the blessed hope and glorious appearing of our great God and Savior Jesus Christ.

—Titus 2:12–13

2. Be watchful and ready for His coming.

Let us be that faithful and wise servant who was found faithful by his master and be ready at all times.

> Watch therefore, for you do not know what hour your Lord is coming. But know this, that if the master of the house had known what hour the thief would come, he would have watched and not allowed his house to be broken into. Therefore you also be ready, for the Son of Man is coming at an hour you do not expect. Who then is a faithful and wise servant, whom his master made ruler over his household, to give them food in due season? Blessed is that servant whom his master, when he comes, will find so doing. Assuredly, I say to you that he will make him ruler over all his goods. But if that evil servant says in his heart, "My master is delaying his coming," and begins to beat his fellow servants, and to eat and drink with the drunkards, the master of that servant will come on a day when he is not looking for him and at an hour that he is not aware of, and will cut him in two and appoint him his portion with the hypocrites. There shall be weeping and gnashing of teeth.
>
> —MATTHEW 24:42–51

3. Love His appearing and receive the crown of righteousness.

> Finally, there is laid up for me the crown of righteousness, which the Lord, the righteous Judge, will give to me on that Day, and not to me only but also to all who have loved His appearing.
>
> —2 TIMOTHY 4:8

4. Be a faithful servant in what you have been given because faithfulness will be rewarded.

For I say to you, that to everyone who has will be given; and from him who does not have, even what he has will be taken away from him.

—LUKE 19:26

5. Let us be found without spot and blameless looking forward to the coming of the Lord.

Therefore, beloved, looking forward to these things, be diligent to be found by Him in peace, without spot and blameless.

—2 PETER 3:14

6. Be found steadfast lest we fall.

You therefore, beloved, since you know this beforehand, beware lest you also fall from your own steadfastness, being led away with the error of the wicked.

—2 PETER 3:17

7. Grow in His grace and knowledge.

Grow in the grace and knowledge of our Lord and Savior Jesus Christ.

—2 PETER 3:18

Beloved, I beheld the archangel ready to blow the trumpet any moment to announce the Lord's return. The second coming of Jesus Christ can happen any minute. Let us be prepared for His sudden return. If you are unsure of your standing in Christ, please repent now and be saved. For it will be terrible to be left behind when He comes.

He who testifies to these things says, "Surely I am coming quickly." Amen. Even so, come, Lord Jesus!

—REVELATION 22:20

Chapter Eighteen

THE IMPACT OF THIS JOURNEY
WITH JESUS CHRIST

THIS JOURNEY THAT began in the year 1995, when I began to accompany Jesus Christ to different parts of hell, has had a deep impact on my life resulting in my complete transformation.

In His light I saw my faults and weaknesses, much to my shame. As I was molded by His truth, the desire for those things I once considered important melted away; and as a result, they hold no meaning today in my life.

> But what things were gain to me, these I have counted loss for Christ. Yet indeed I also count all things loss for the excellence of the knowledge of Christ Jesus my Lord, for whom I have suffered the loss of all things, and count them as rubbish, that I may gain Christ and be found in Him, not having my own righteousness, which is from the law, but that which is through faith in Christ, the righteousness which is from God by faith; that I may know Him and the power of His resurrection, and the fellowship of His sufferings, being conformed to His death.
>
> —PHILIPPIANS 3:7–10

This life-changing journey taught me the following valuable lessons:

1. We are accountable to God.

I saw and understood that life is a gift from God and there is a unique purpose of God behind each life. It is never about us but all about God for His glory. The breath of God that gives us life is His grace, and therefore we are indebted to live this life to proclaim His goodness.

We have been created to be in communion with Him, and we need to do so by worshipping Him in spirit and truth.

Each one of us is unique and blessed with specific talents. Therefore, we are also accountable to God—the Giver—as to what we do with these talents.

2. Pride fades with death.

Priorities in life that cause pride and divide mankind while alive, such as wealth, worldly accomplishments, color of the skin, etc., cease with death. No matter how popular, successful, and rich we have been in this world, if we do not have Jesus in our lives, we will be the poorest of the poor after our death. The one and only thing that really matters after death is how important Jesus was in our lives and what we did for Him.

Our intellect, fame, personal achievements, wealth, wisdom, etc., mean nothing once we are dead; and we will regret what we held dear and prided about when alive. Witnessing the lost souls of once world-renowned personalities to the common lost souls in hell, I learned this lesson that no matter what the matter of pride in this life, it will fade away with death.

3. The object of pride is an idol.

The matter of pride results in idol worship that takes us away far from God. As I saw those lost souls in hell well-known universally for their talents, I noticed that idol worshipping their talents on earth took them far away from God. Those souls had placed their talents as a matter of pride above God and landed in hell.

Beloved, is there something in life that you are proud about? Do you look down on others as a result of that? No matter what it may be, that object of pride in your life is an idol; and idol worship is unacceptable to God. Break your idols and repent.

Talent is not to be worshipped but used for God's glory, not for self. The Bible instructs:

> And whatever you do in word or deed, do all in the name of the Lord Jesus, giving thanks to God the Father through Him.
>
> —COLOSSIANS 3:17

4. The enemy backs off when he sees the truth of God's Word in our lives.

My eyes were opened to this truth that victory in the battle with the enemy comes only by the indwelling richness of God's Word in our life and living by it.

> For the word of God is living and powerful, and sharper than any two-edged sword, piercing even to the division of soul and spirit, and of joints and marrow, and is a discerner of the thoughts and intents of the heart.
>
> —HEBREWS 4:12

The Word of God, if not accepted in totality and applied to ourself just as given by God, is rendered ineffective against the powerful schemes of the enemy. This God's Word—referred to as the truth—is a powerful sword of the Spirit (Eph. 6:17) when we live and practice this truth. Jesus overcame the tempter with this sword of the Spirit (Matt. 4:11). I witnessed Satan laugh at those Christians who attempted to fight him while twisting the Word of God for their own benefit or not accepting it in its totality.

We need to understand that we are dealing with a powerful enemy and Jesus Christ has defeated him. Therefore, we prevail against Satan our enemy only through Jesus Christ and not through our own efforts. If we fail to live by the truth of God's Word, it results in being defeated by the enemy while alive and lost after death. I beheld many souls languishing in hell because they erred in accepting and applying the Word of God as written in their practical lives.

Numerous trips to hell have opened my eyes to this fact that there is no fooling with God's Word and it has to be handled accurately to prevail against the enemy. The power of God lies in the truth of His Word, and the enemy backs off when he sees this truth in our lives.

5. The Savior's compassion is beyond comprehension.

I beheld Jesus Christ weep over lost sinners many times. I was moved to see such deep compassion of the Messiah for the lost. He told me over and over again, "I wanted to save them. If only they would have asked Me to wash their sins, I would have done so and they will not be found in hell today; but they rejected Me." It hurt Him so much that a lost soul was not willing to be saved while alive and ended up in hell. They need not have been in hell if only they had accepted Him as their Savior.

God in His mercy does not desire any soul to perish and gives chances to repent. I did not see any lost soul in hell who was not given any opportunity on earth to repent.

Impacted by the love of Jesus, my burden, commitment, and passion to see the unsaved saved has increased.

6. The Savior has great humility.

What is man that you are mindful of him, And the son of man that You visit him?

—PSALM 8:4

This journey opened my eyes to the humility of the merciful Savior. I beheld Him in His majesty and power with all things subject to Him; yet this King of kings walked beside me—an undeserving candidate in all my weaknesses—and showed me those parts of hell. His humility taught me to submit to Him, the great Teacher, and attain wisdom.

    7. My ministry is impacted.

This journey with Christ has brought me much closer to Him and increased my gifting by leaps and bounds. Apart from the many who have come to the saving knowledge of Jesus Christ and have committed their lives for this cause, I have also witnessed supernatural deliverances and healings in the ministry.

Chapter Nineteen

A NOTE TO THE READER

ELL IS A real place of unending affliction, as you have just read. It is important to make a decision regarding where you will spend your eternity. Reader, are you prepared for death if it were to strike you now? Where will you spend your eternity? Hell is a reality and so is Satan. If you do not have the assurance that your sins are forgiven, then you are on your way to hell. The good news is that you do not have to go there. Right now you have an opportunity to repent and be saved by Jesus Christ.

Possibly you have questions about God that nobody can answer. I had questions, too. Reader, I found my answers in Him; and you will too, if you will just give Him a chance.

Reader, I did not become a Christian because someone forced me to. It is only because Jesus Christ revealed Himself to me.

I had two choices in front of me; the world and its charms were beckoning me on one hand, and the other was a deep need within me that only God could fulfill. One day I was desperate to know the truth about Jesus—whether He really existed, and if He did, did He really care about me—His creation? I blurted out, "Jesus, if You love me, show it to me." I did not know that God would dramatically prove Himself to me the very next day.

God sent me the message of His love through a complete stranger. Right after I was back from school, there was a knock on my door. A stranger stood outside the door and asked for me. The stranger explained that God had given him the directions to my house plus my name and sent him with a special message to be delivered to me.

As I met with this unknown visitor to receive the message he had brought me, this is what he said to me: "Jesus Christ sent me here to tell you that He loves you." Then he went on to tell me that I had asked this of Jesus at a certain time the day before.

It was impossible for this stranger, whom I had never seen before, to know that since I had never shared this with anyone at all. It had to be somebody who could read my thoughts, who knew everything about me.

Who could possibly know everything about me so precisely—my name, my address, the thoughts known only to me, and the exact timing of the question? The one person who fit the bill was God Himself. As this powerful reality struck me, the scales fell off my eyes. "'Is not My word like a fire?' says the LORD, "'And like a hammer that breaks the rock in pieces?'" (Jer. 23:29).

Beloved, the truth of the love of God compelled me to seek Him and as a result I desired to be born again. I wanted this God who cared for me so much and understood me perfectly. He was the One who had created me and who knew me better than myself. "Your hands have made me and fashioned me" (Ps. 119:73).

I was a "see it to believe it" person, and God proved Himself to me. Bowled over by His great love and mercy, I accepted Jesus as my Savior. After this born-again experience, later that night I was also baptized in the Holy Spirit, as mentioned in Acts 2.

> When the Day of Pentecost had fully come, they were all with one accord in one place. And suddenly there came a sound from heaven, as of a rushing mighty wind, and it filled the whole house where they were sitting. Then there appeared to them divided tongues, as of fire, and *one* sat upon each of them. And they were all filled with the Holy Spirit and began to speak with other tongues, as the Spirit gave them utterance.
>
> —ACTS 2:1–4

After this experience I picked up the Bible after many months of disuse. Dusting the dirt off the Bible that had gathered over months,

I held the Bible in my hands and prayed, "Dear Holy Spirit, please teach me the Word of God." And from that time the Bible finally began to make sense to me and I began to understand the Word of God for the very first time in my life under the teaching of the Holy Spirit. Since that moment, my life has never been the same.

God may not answer your questions as dramatically as He did for me. But just as He sent that stranger to convey His message of love to me, I come to you, a perfect stranger, conveying the very same message of His love. Please, do not reject His love for you.

Do you feel there is nobody out there in this world who cares for you and that nobody loves you? Let me tell you that Jesus loves you. I have tasted of His love and found Him sweeter than honey (Ps. 119:103; 19:10). I invite you to "taste and see that the LORD is good" (34:8).

There are some who are being taken advantage of in the name of love. Beloved, love is about selfless giving. You will find that love you have been looking for only in Jesus Christ and not elsewhere. He cares for you so much that He offered Himself selflessly on the cross, to redeem you from your sins. The Bible says, "Yes, I have loved you with an everlasting love; Therefore with lovingkindness I have drawn you" (Jer. 31:3).

Have you gone away far from God for some reason? Did somebody you look up to let you down? No man or woman is perfect; hence I urge you to look only at Jesus Christ, the perfect One. No matter what the cause may be of your backsliding, please come back to Him. Similar to the father who in love received his son who went away when he came back (mentioned in the following parable), God is waiting for you to come back to Him.

> And he arose and came to his father. But when he was still a great way off, his father saw him and had compassion, and ran and fell on his neck and kissed him. And the son said to him, "Father, I have sinned against heaven and in your sight, and am no longer worthy to be called your son."

But the father said to his servants, "Bring out the best robe and put it on him, and put a ring on his hand and sandals on his feet. And bring the fatted calf here and kill it, and let us eat and be merry; for this my son was dead and is alive again; he was lost and is found." And they began to be merry.

—LUKE 15:20–24

No matter what you have done or how far you have slipped away from Him, God will pardon you if you truly repent and forsake the evil way. God the Father seeks a loving relationship with you. If you draw close to Him, He will draw close to you, according to His promise, and He will manifest Himself to you if you love Him. "Draw near to God and He will draw near to you" (James 4:8).

He who has My commandments and keeps them, it is he who loves Me. And he who loves Me will be loved by My Father, and I will love him and manifest Myself to him.

—JOHN 14:21

You need to make space for Him in your hustle and bustle of life to learn, listen, and receive what He has for you. Let not the cacophony of the distractions of the world silence God's gentle voice speaking in your spirit. So make sure that you do not cram your life with the love of things of the world.

Beloved, do not be deceived by the enemy that there is no hell. In this world we are governed by a system and bound to follow that system. Failure to follow can result in us being penalized. Therefore, it is naïve to think that the great God who rules the universe would not run it in order. Hence, you *are* accountable for your actions to God. Whatever you sow, you will also reap. If you sow according to the flesh you will die but you sow for God you will reap an everlasting life (Gal. 6:7–8).

God does not condone sin. The Bible says, "The soul who sins shall die" (Ezek. 18:20). The consequence of sin is death. God in

His mercy made a provision for us—sinners—in His Son Jesus Christ: "The blood of Jesus Christ His Son cleanses us from all sin" (1 John 1:7).

If you do not repent and die in your sins, you will certainly end up in hell: "But he who does wrong will be repaid for what he has done, and there is no partiality" (Col. 3:25).

God desires you to seek life and live.

> I call heaven and earth as witnesses today against you, that I have set before you life and death, blessing and cursing; therefore choose life, that both you and your descendants may live.
>
> —Deuteronomy 30:19

Only Jesus Christ can fill that vacuum in your life. It can never be filled with fame, riches, power, or even earthly love. Therefore, seek Him for He can be found, if you search for Him with all your heart, according to His promise in Jeremiah 29:13.

I sincerely hope that you will receive this message in the light of God's Word and not reject His plea. If you choose to accept Jesus Christ today—the Giver of life—even if you were to die, you will live, according to His Word.

> I am the resurrection and the life. He who believes in Me, though he may die, he shall live.
>
> —John 11:25

Chapter Twenty

STEPS TO PRACTICAL CHRISTIAN LIVING

S IN ALIENATES ONE from eternal life, resulting in eternal condemnation in hell. On the other hand, repentance of sins assures eternal life of joy in heaven. Beloved, it is important to understand that God looks right through you—the "real" you hidden to the world but open before God. Christian living begins with getting rid of the mask of pretension and coming to Jesus just as you are. Confessing your sins and accepting Jesus as your Savior results in being born again.

> For with the heart one believes unto righteousness, and with the mouth confession is made unto salvation.
> —ROMANS 10:10

It is important to maintain this living relationship with Christ after being born again. I have laid down a few steps that will help you in your spiritual walk with Christ.

- Step 1: Obey the Lord in baptism.

After you are born again, obey the Lord in baptism. This is a proclamation of your death to the world and being alive in Jesus Christ.

- Step 2: Desire to be rooted in Christ.

Have regular quiet time by devoting time to read the Bible and meditate on it. Receiving help from a mature believer in Jesus Christ is an added blessing.

- Step 3: Practice holiness.

Be holy, "without which no one will see the Lord" (Heb. 12:14).

- Step 4: Seek to be filled by His Holy Spirit.

When the Day of Pentecost had fully come, they were all with one accord in one place. And suddenly there came a sound from heaven, as of a rushing mighty wind, and it filled the whole house where they were sitting. Then there appeared to them divided tongues, as of fire, and one sat upon each of them. And they were all filled with the Holy Spirit and began to speak with other tongues, as the Spirit gave them utterance.

—ACTS 2:1–4

The Holy Spirit helps us to live victoriously in this sinful world, "likewise the Spirit also helps in our weaknesses" (Rom. 8:26).

- Step 5: Start attending a Bible-believing church and fellowship with like-minded Christians.

This will help you to grow spiritually in the Lord and understand His love for you more. Attend regular Bible study and prayers with those who share the same beliefs and convictions as you.

- Step 6: Do not be entangled again with the bondage of sin.

God has set you free from this bondage of sin; going back to a life of sin is dangerous and it will result in perdition.

> Stand fast therefore in the liberty by which Christ has
> made us free, and do not be entangled again with a yoke
> of bondage.
>
> —GALATIANS 5:1

If you follow the above-mentioned steps, issues of living water will flow out of you and you will not only escape hell but also save others from hell.

Remember, Jesus loves you and does not want you to go to hell. Accept Him or reject Him. The choice is yours.

> God did not send His Son into the world to condemn the
> world, but that the world through Him might be saved.
>
> —JOHN 3:17

ABOUT THE AUTHOR

SHRADHA S. PHILIP is an ordained pastor and has served in India and internationally. An anointed speaker much in demand, the presence of God is emphasized in all her meetings, resulting in supernatural conversions, mighty deliverances, and healing. Convicted by their encounter with God, many are serving today in full-time ministry.

Shradha has been awarded an honorary doctorate in recognition of her ministry. She is the founder of Warriors in Christ Ministries. She is also the author of *She Was Born to Live*.

CONTACT THE AUTHOR

www.warriorsinchrist.org

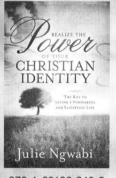
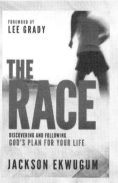

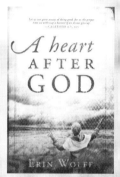